Cow And Humanity
Made For Each Other

By
Dr. Sahadeva dasa

B.COM., ACA., ICWA., PHD
Chartered Accountant

Soul Science University Press
www.cowism.com

"By eliminating beef from the human diet, our species takes a significant step toward a new species consciousness, reaching out in a spirit of shared partnership with the bovine, and, by extension, other sentient creatures with whom we share the earth."   -Jeremy Rifkin

Readers interested in the subject matter of this
book are invited to correspond with the publisher at:
SoulScienceUniversity@gmail.com +91 98490 95990

To order a copy write to chandra@rgbooks.co.in
or buy online: at www.rgbooks.co.in

First Edition: September 2009

Soul Science University Press expresses its gratitude to the Bhaktivedanta Book
Trust International (BBT), for the use of quotes by His Divine Grace
A.C.Bhaktivedanta Swami Prabhupada.
Copyright Bhaktivedanta Book Trust International (BBT)

ISBN 978-81-909760-3-9

Price in India: Rs.100/-

Published by:
Dr. Sahadeva dasa for Soul Science University Press

Printed by:
Rainbow Print Pack, Hyderabad

Dedicated to....

His Divine Grace A.C.Bhaktivedanta Swami Prabhupada

The basic principle of economic development is centered on land and cows. The necessities of human society are food grains, fruits, milk, minerals, clothing, wood, etc. One requires all these items to fulfill the material needs of the body. ...During the regime of Maharaja Yudhisthira, all over the world there were regulated rainfalls. Rainfalls are not in the control of the human being. ...Not only do regulated rains help ample production of grains and fruits, but when they combine with astronomical influences there is ample production of valuable stones and pearls. Grains and vegetables can sumptuously feed a man and animals, and a fatty cow delivers enough milk to supply a man sumptuously with vigor and vitality. If there is enough milk, enough grains, enough fruit, enough cotton, enough silk and enough jewels, then why do the people need cinemas, houses of prostitution, slaughterhouses, etc.? What is the need of an artificial luxurious life of cinema, cars, radio, flesh and hotels? Has this civilization produced anything but quarreling individually and nationally? Has this civilization enhanced the cause of equality and fraternity by sending thousands of men into a hellish factory and the war fields at the whims of a particular man?

It is said here that the cows used to moisten the pasturing land with milk because their milk bags were fatty and the animals were joyful. Do they not require, therefore, proper protection for a joyful life by being fed with a sufficient quantity of grass in the field? Why should men kill cows for their selfish purposes? Why should man not be satisfied with grains, fruits and milk, which, combined together, can produce hundreds and thousands of palatable dishes. Why are there slaughterhouses all over the world to kill innocent animals? Maharaja Parikshit, grandson of Maharaja Yudhisthira, while touring his vast kingdom, saw a black man attempting to kill a cow. The King at once arrested the butcher and chastised him sufficiently. Should not a king or executive head protect the lives of the poor animals who are unable to defend themselves? Is this humanity? Are not the animals of a country citizens also? Then why are they allowed to be butchered in organized slaughterhouses? Are these the signs of equality, fraternity and nonviolence?

- Srila Prabhupada
(Srimad Bhagavatam 1.10.4)

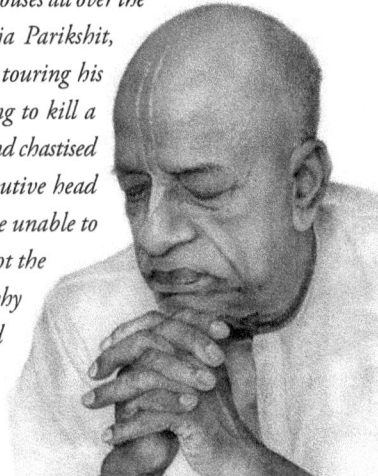

By The Same Author

Oil - Final Countdown To A Global Crisis And Its Solutions

End of Modern Civilization and Alternative Future

To Kill Cow Means To End Human Civilization

Capitalism Communism And Cowism - A New Economics For The 21st Century

Cows Are Cool - Love 'Em !

Wondrous Glories of Vraja

Modern Foods - Stealing Years From Your Life

Noble Cow - Munching Grass, Looking Curious And Just Hanging Around

Lets Be Friends - A Curious, Calm Cow

We Feel - Just Like You Do

(More information on availability at the back)

Contents

Preface

We're finally going to get the bill for the Industrial Age. If the projections are right, it's going to be a big one: the ecological collapse of the planet, says Jeremy Rifkin. At the dawn of the industrial age two hundred years ago, we took a wrong turn when we started living on nature's capital instead of nature's incomes. We started gorging upon resources that took nature millions of years to create. These resources were saved up by nature according to its own plan of functioning.

Nature has her own way; she better understands her own affairs than we. We have one planet to live on and all our needs have to be satisfied with whatever is in here. We can not import a thing from other planets for our survival, no matter how much we advertise our dubious moon missions. All we can do is blow up billions and console the taxpayers with few rocks.

This senseless exploitation of resources can not go on forever. This cradle to grave economics in which we turn every natural resource into a toxic waste is inherently unsustainable. In nature, there is no such thing as waste. So called waste generated by one living being is effectively utilized by another and so on until nothing is left. This is called the cycle of life. But today our linear system of living has replaced this natural cyclical system.

This is where cow comes into picture. Living with cow is living on nature's incomes without depleting its capital resources. Modern civilization is utilizing nature's capital resources. These resources like petroleum were accumulated by nature over millions of years, but we have squandered them in just 150 years. How long this reckless lifestyle will go on? In Vedic tradition, cow provided all the necessities of human society. Society reciprocated her services by protecting her. Bull was regarded as a symbol of religion and also a father because bull produced grains by ploughing the fields. Now we have tractors and other agricultural machinery but once the oil runs out, we will have to revert back to bulls again (if any left by the time).

In the universal scheme of creation, fate of species called humans has been attached to that of another, namely cows, to an absolute and overwhelming degree. This implies that welfare and well-being of cows leads to progress and prosperity and mistreatment of cows results in degradation of society.

In the natural plan of Vedic living, human society depends on cows for its requirements of economic prosperity, food production, soil fertility, nutrition, healthcare, fuel supply, transport, spiritual well-being, sustainable development, individual and social peace, higher consciousness, development of human qualities, performance of religious duties, environmental protection, ecological preservation, advancement of art & culture, cottage industry etc.

Many of the maladies staring in our face today can be traced to this factor – humanity distancing itself from the timeless culture of cow protection.

Sahadeva dasa

Dr. Sahadeva dasa
1st October 2009
Secunderabad

1.

Cow Is Complete Ecology
Cow Represents Life & Earth

On Tuesday, June 2, 2009, from 9:00 PM to 11:00 PM, millions around the world watched a television program called Earth 2100. It was presented by American Broadcasting Company (ABC) and hosted by ABC journalist Bob Woodruff. The two-hour special explored what a worst-case future might look like if humans do not take action on current or impending problems that could threaten civilization. The problems addressed in the program included climate change, food insecurity and misuse of energy resources.

We have been given a planet to live on. In the end, cockroaches would prove to be more intelligent than humans if humans destroy themselves. Intelligence is really a survival skill for the entire species and that which survives proves intelligent on a species level.

The program included predictions of a dystopian Earth in the years 2015, 2030, 2050, 2085, and 2100 by scientists, historians, social anthropologists, and economists, including Jared Diamond, Thomas Homer-Dixon, Peter Gleick, James Howard Kunstler, Heidi Cullen,

> *Nothing will benefit human health and increase chances for survival of life on Earth as much as the evolution to a vegetarian diet.*
> *~Albert Einstein*

and Joseph Tainter.

According to Executive Producer Michael Bicks, the program was developed to show the worst-case scenario for human civilization. Again, its not that these events will happen dot on time — rather, that if we fail to seriously address the complex problems of climate change, resource depletion and food security, they are much more likely to happen.

Earth 2100 : The Final Century of Civilization?

Planet is at Risk and experts warn that factors like food insecurity, resource depletion, climate change could bring catastrophe in next century. It's an idea that most of us would rather not face -- that within the next century, life as we know it could come to an end. Our civilization could crumble, leaving only traces of modern human existence behind.

To change the future, first we have to perceive it and in order to plan for the worst, we must anticipate it. It seems outlandish, extreme - even impossible. But according to cutting edge scientific research, it is a very real possibility. And unless we make drastic changes now, it could very well happen.

Experts are giving a stark warning that unless we change course, these issues have the potential to converge in the next century with catastrophic results.

The Future: It's Nearer Than We Think

By 2018, experts predict alternative energy solutions that are currently in their infancy will gain momentum. But will it be enough? In 2018, global demand for fossil fuels could be massive and growing, but experts say oil will be harder to find and more expensive to

I am the earth. You are the earth. The Earth is dying. You and I are dying and You and I are the murderers. ~ Ymber Delecto

We are making progress, just wait!

consume.

Michael Klare, professor of peace and world security studies at Hampshire College says, "We have no new source of energy on the horizon that's currently capable of being developed on a large enough scale to replace the supply of oil in any near-term framework." If the cost of gasoline skyrockets, few may be able to afford to maintain the lifestyles to which we've grown accustomed. But will that convince us to change our ways? A really deep change is required in the ways we think and do things in life.

A House On Fire - Earth And Environment Are Burning

The Wheels of Progress Are Crushing The World

The environment is burning worldwide. But there is no fire escape here, there is no emergency exit here. We are confined within the walls of this earthly atmosphere and have no place to run to. Blazing fires of air pollution, water pollution, energy crisis, food insecurity,

> *Don't blow it - good planets are hard to find.*
> *- Quoted in Time*

toxic waste, acid rains, rising temperatures, melting ice, nuclear waste, pesticides, violence, wars, mounting trash, soil loss, water crisis, biodiversity loss, rainforest destruction, ozone layer depletion, environmental warfare, are scorching our lives, scalding our planet.

When it comes to human history, the themes of civilizations rising and falling repeats itself ad nauseum. This collapse occurs mostly when the civilizations fail to take into account their environment and when there comes a point where the growth and need for resources outstrip what their environment can provide. Compared to the rest of human history, our story will be no different. When the environments in which preceding cultures flourished failed to support their needs, these civilizations collapsed. Why should our civilization be any different? Such an environmental collapse brought down the Minoans, the Indus Valley people, Mesopotamia, Egypt and the Hsieh Kingdoms, to name a few.

When the land failed to provide, people moved to where they thought there was better land and even fought the current occupants for that land. Today also, due to climatic changes, many parts of the world like Australia, Africa, parts of Asia and Europe are facing increasing desertification. Redistribution of rainfall is taking place and it can have dangerous implications for world's food supply. Climatic changes have always taken place and the world has always changed but the scale at which things are happening is scary. Human history is littered with numerous examples to support this idea. In Meso America, the Maya and Anasazi peoples found their existences endangered as their crops failed and the Sonoran desert advanced north into what is now Colorado, Utah, New Mexico and Arizona.

They are thinking it is paradise. And the paradise is lost every ten years or fifteen years by the bombing. German bombs the France, and France bombs the... This is their paradise. So let them understand that "You are all fools. You are fool's paradise. This is life, what we are doing." Teach them so that the fools will understand what is life. They are manufacturing atom bomb.
-Srila Prabhupada (Morning Walk, June 17, 1974, Germany)

Western civilization, which is a world civilization now is on the decline. The problems that precipitated this decline could be traced to the 18th Century, when some of the countries started importing resources from far-flung parts of the earth, to fuel the industrial revolution back home. They grew so accustomed to it that they became interdependent on the steady flow of these resources coming to them. However, they failed to consider what kind of resources it took to get those resources and that was probably their undoing. This was the dawn of an era of overconsumption and greed, an era of colonization and exploitation. People that can not feed itself off of what they produce will fail. They either move, die out, or resort to warfare to get what they want or a combination of all of these. In the last few decades also, we have seen this scenario play itself in various parts of the world.

Culture of Animal Eating - Lying At The Heart of Resource Depletion, Overconsumption and Environmental Destruction

Most destructive aspect of industrial revolution was reflected in changes in dietary habits of whole nations. People steadily moved up the food chain, from a staple of bread, potato and cheese to beef, pork and lamb. But many did not care for the price tag attached to such extravagance, except for some sensible souls like Einstein who remarked, "Nothing will benefit human health and increase chances for survival of life on Earth as much as the evolution to a vegetarian diet." This wasn't coming from an old hat but from the most prominent scientist of modern era. Even in recent times, experts such as Dr. Neal Barnard duly warn us, "The beef industry has contributed to more American deaths than all the wars of this century, all natural disasters, and all automobile accidents combined. If beef is your idea of "real food for real people", you'd better live real close to a real good hospital."

The earth we abuse and the living things we kill will, in the end, take their revenge; for in exploiting their presence we are diminishing our future.
- Marya Mannes

Thus killing animals for food, fur, leather, and cosmetics is one of the most environmentally destructive practices taking place on the earth today.

The meat industry is linked to deforestation, desertification, water pollution, water shortages, air pollution, and soil erosion. Dr. Neal Barnard, president of the Physicians Committee for Responsible Medicine (USA), therefore says, "If you're a meat eater, you are contributing to the destruction of the environment, whether you know it or not. Clearly the best thing you can do for the Earth is to not support animal agriculture."

And Jeremy Rifkin warns in his widely read book *Beyond Beef*: "Today, millions of Americans, Europeans, and Japanese are consuming countless hamburgers, steaks, and roasts, oblivious to the impact their dietary habits are having on the biosphere and the very survivability of life on earth. Every pound of grain-fed flesh is secured at the expense of a burned forest, an eroded rangeland, a barren field, a dried-up river or stream, and the release of millions of tons of carbon dioxide, nitrous oxide, and methane into the skies."

When We Kill Animals, We Kill The Earth, We Kill Ourselves

Right now we raise about 40 billion animals for food. Animal based diet is leading to a global health crisis unparalleled in human history.

Dietary advice on the subject of global warming and environmental health was never as definitive as it is today. The United Nations has called on governments and individuals to open their eyes to climate change, calling it "the most serious challenge facing the human race." More than any other factor, how we meet that challenge will depend on what we eat.

Meat Eaters Devouring Forests, Destroying Ecosystems

A tree is our most intimate contact with nature and forests form the life line of Earth's atmosphere. In last two centuries, over 90% of

We do not inherit the earth from our ancestors, we borrow it from our children. - Native American Proverb

Growth
Progress
Development

the Earth's forests have been butchered and this is one of the most prominent feature of modern ecocidal policies.

You want to save forests? Just stop eating meat! Each person who becomes a vegetarian saves one acre of trees per year. According to *Vegetarian Times,* half of the annual destruction of tropical rain forests is caused by clearing land for beef cattle ranches. Each pound of hamburger made from Central American or South American beef costs about 55 square feet of rain forest vegetation. Forests all over the world are being cut so that Americans, Europeans and Japanese can have their hamburgers. Its a criminal waste of precious resources.

In the United States, about 260 million acres of forest have been cleared for a meat-centered diet. About 40% of the land in the western United States is used for grazing beef cattle. This has had a detrimental effect on wildlife.

About a fifth of the world's land is used for grazing meat animals - twice the area used for growing crops. Because of the deforestation, soil erosion and desertification meat industry causes, it is fundamentally unsustainable and has an extremely negative impact on the environment. Thirty percent of the earth's land is now occupied by livestock, with another 33 percent devoted to GMO feed crops, and this number is expanding every year. Seventy percent of previously forested land in the Amazon has been converted into cropland and pastures, destroying biodiversity, introducing carcinogenic pesticides, and playing a primary role in pushing species toward extinction at a rate 500 times of that we ought to be experiencing according to models based on fossil records.

Inevitably, intensive animal agriculture depletes valuable natural resources. Instead of being eaten by people, the vast majority of grains harvested is fed to farm animals. For this wasteful and inefficient practice, agribusinesses exploit vast stretches of land. Forests, wetlands, and other natural ecosystems and wildlife habitats have been decimated. Scarce fossil fuels, groundwater, and topsoil resources which took millenium to develop are now disappearing. Of all agricultural land in the United States, 80-87% is now used to raise animals for food.

They are misusing these trees by cutting, manufacturing paper, heaps of paper, in each house throwing daily. They do not read, but they are supplied heaps of paper and cutting these trees. Simply waste. Now wood and paper shortage all over the world. It takes so much time to grow, and one day they cut hundreds of trees like this and put into the paper mill. And heaps of paper is given every house, and he throws away. Then you bring garbage tank. In this way, waste.
-Srila Prabhupada (Walk Around New Talavan Farm, August 1, 1975, New Orleans)

The space equivalent to seven football fields is being destroyed in rainforests every minute; 50 million acres of tropical forest in Latin America alone have been cut down for livestock production since 1970. In Canada also, local wilderness is being destroyed for more and more grazing land for livestock.

Meat Eating - The Cause For World Hunger & Criminal Waste of Grains

There is plenty of food. It is just not reaching human stomachs. Of the 2.13bn tonnes consumed in 2008, only 1.01bn, according to the UN's Food and Agriculture Organisation (FAO), reached people. The rest was used up by meat industry and biofuel industry.

The great food recession is sweeping the world faster than the credit crunch. The price of rice has risen by three-quarters in the past year, that of wheat by 130%. There are food crises in 37 countries. One hundred million people, according to the World Bank, could be pushed into deeper poverty by the high prices. But at 2.1bn tonnes,

last year's global grain harvest broke all records. It beat the previous year's by almost 5%. If hunger can strike now, what will happen if harvests decline?

While 100 million tonnes of food will be diverted this year to feed cars, 760 million tonnes will be snatched from the mouths of humans to feed animals. *This could cover the global food deficit 14 times.* If we care about hunger, we have to eat less meat.

Traditionally, most societies would eat meat only on special occasions unless it was a hunting, foraging tribe. Meat as staple diet is unknown in any traditional culture.

It is depressing to consider that throughout the last big famine in Ethiopia, the country was exporting desperately needed soy to Europe to feed farmed animals. The same relationship held true throughout the famine in Somalia in the early 1990's. The same relationship holds between Latin America and the United States today. As an example, two-thirds of the agriculturally productive land in Central America is devoted to raising farmed animals, who are exported or eaten by the wealthy few in these countries.

The world's cattle alone consume a quantity of food equal to the caloric needs of 8.7 billion people -- more than the entire human population on Earth. Meanwhile, the UN says that 1000 million people are suffering from "nutritional deficiency" (i.e. they're starving).

Thus more than half of the world's grain is consumed by animals

As soon as you make misuse, the supply will be stopped. After all, the supply is not in your control. You cannot manufacture all these things. You can kill thousands of cows daily, but you cannot generate even one ant. And you are very much proud of your science. You see. Just produce one ant in the laboratory, moving, with independence. And you are killing so many animals? Why? So how long this will go on? Everything will be stopped. Just like a child. Mother is giving good, nice foodstuff, and he's spoiling. So what the mother will do? "All right. From tomorrow you'll not get." That is natural.
(Srila Prabhupada, Lecture, Bhagavad-gita 3.11-19 — Los Angeles, December 27, 1968)

that are later slaughtered for meat. *Meat production is a very inefficient process. It takes 16 pounds of grain and soybeans to produce 1 pound of feedlot beef.* If people were to subsist on grains and other vegetarian foods alone, this would put far less strain on the earth's agricultural lands. About 20 vegetarians can be fed from the land it takes to feed 1 meat eater. During the process of converting grain to meat, 90% of the protein, 99% of the carbohydrates, and 100% of the dietary fiber are lost.

Eighty percent of the corn raised in the United States is fed to livestock, as well as 95% of the oats. Altogether, 56% of all agricultural land in the United States is used for beef production. If all the soybeans and grain fed yearly to US livestock were set aside for human consumption, it would feed 1.3 billion people.

In his book "Proteins: Their Chemistry and Politics," Dr. Aaron Altshul notes that, "In terms of calorie units per acre, a diet of grains, vegetables and beans will support twenty times more people than a diet of meat.

If the earth's arable land were used primarily for the production of vegetarian foods, the planet could easily support a population of

twenty billion and more.

In a report submitted to the United Nations World Food Conference (Rome, 1974), Rene Durmont, an agricultural economist at France's National Agricultural Institute, made this judgement, "The over consumption of meat by the rich means hunger for the poor."

Really, it comes down to this: generating meat for human consumption requires vast amounts of land that could be used to feed people, and is therefore withholding food from millions of starving people.

Soil Erosion and Desertification

Bad soil is bad for global health, and the evidence is mounting that the world' soil is in trouble. We're dead without good soil. Soil holds minerals and organic compounds critical to life. Without good soil we have got nothing.

All over the world, more than seven and a half million acres of soil has been degraded. That's larger than the U.S. and Canada combined. What remains is ailing as a result of compaction, erosion and salination making it near impossible to plant and adding to greenhouse gases and air pollution. Soil degradation is putting the

Ample food grains can be produced through agricultural enterprises, and profuse supplies of milk, yogurt and ghee can be arranged through cow protection. Abundant honey can be obtained if the forests are protected. Unfortunately, in modern civilization, men are busy killing the cows that are the source of yogurt, milk and ghee, they are cutting down all the trees that supply honey, and they are opening factories to manufacture nuts, bolts, automobiles and wine instead of engaging in agriculture. How can the people be happy? They must suffer from all the misery of materialism. Their bodies become wrinkled and gradually deteriorate until they become almost like dwarves, and a bad odor emanates from their bodies because of unclean perspiration resulting from eating all kinds of nasty things. This is not human civilization. If people actually want happiness in this life and want to prepare for the best in the next life, they must adopt a Vedic civilization.
-Srila Prabhupada (Srimad Bhagavatam 5.16.25)

future of the global population is at risk according to a National Geographic article by Charles Mann.

Civil unrest in Latin America, Asia and Africa have been attributed to a lack of food and affordable food as a result of poor soil. *Currently, only 11-percent of the world's land feeds six billion people.*

Experts estimate that by 2030 the Earth's population will reach 8.3 billion. Farmers will need to increase food production by 40-percent. But not much soil remains.

Scientists don't know much and don't care either about this critical resource.

Overgrazing and the intensive production of feed grain for cattle and other meat animals results in high levels of soil erosion. According to Alan B. Durning of the Worldwatch Institute (1986), one pound of beef from cattle raised on feedlots represents the loss of 35 pounds of topsoil. Over the past few centuries, the United States has lost about two-thirds of its topsoil.

In other countries, such as Australia and the nations of Africa on the southern edge of the Sahara, cattle grazing and feed-crop production on marginal lands contribute substantially to desertification.

Unprecedented Air Pollution

Burning of oil in the production of feed grain results in air pollution, including carbon dioxide, the main cause of global warming. Another major source of air pollution is the burning of tropical forests to clear land for cattle grazing.

The meat industry burns up a lot of fossil fuel, pouring pollutants into the air. Calorie for calorie, it takes 39 times more energy to produce beef than soybeans. *The petroleum used in the United States would decrease by 60% if people adopted a vegetarian diet, as per Vegetarian Times, 1990.*

And in their book *For the Common Good,* World Bank economist Herman E. Daly and philosopher John B. Cobb, Jr., say, "If a simple and healthful change in eating habits along with localization of most food production and a major shift toward organic farming were to take place over the next generation, food production and distribution could be weaned from their current heavy dependence on fossil fuels. In the process, the enormous suffering now inflicted on livestock would be greatly reduced."

The meat industry, in addition to producing carbon dioxide, is also responsible for other greenhouse gases, such as methane. Methane is produced directly by the digestive system of grain fed cows. This greenhouse gas is considered very dangerous because each molecule of methane traps 20 times more heat than a molecule of carbon dioxide.

Cows are being fed unnatural diet of soya, corn and host of other grains. Cows do need grains but in very small quantities. By nature's way, cows are meant to live on grass and vegetation. Each year about 500 million tons of methane enter the atmosphere, contributing about

They are now killing animal, but animal lives on this grass and grains. When there will be no grass, no grains, where they will get animal? They'll kill their own son and eat. That time is coming. Nature's law is that you grow your own food. But they are not interested in growing food. They are interested in manufacturing bolts and nuts.
-Srila Prabhupada *(Morning Walk — June 22, 1974, Germany)*

18% of the total greenhouse gases. Cows which are kept in feedlots and force-fed artificially, account for 60 million tons of the methane, about 12%. Therefore, methane emitted by feedlot cows amounts to 2% of the total greenhouse gas emissions.

In India, there are about 270 million cows, but 99.9% of them are range fed.

Water Pollution And Grave Threat To Water Supply

In the context of the global water supply, the impact of animal agriculture threatens utter catastrophe. Every kilo of beef requires 16,000 litres of water, according to the Institute for Water Education. This means a single person can save more water simply by not eating a pound of beef than they could by not showering for an entire year. Factory farming is responsible for 37 percent of pesticide contamination, 50 percent of antibiotic contamination and one-third

Modern technology
Owes ecology
An apology.
-Alan M. Eddison

15

of the nitrogen and phosphorus loads found in freshwater. Nearly half of all water consumed in the developed countries is used to raise animals for food.

Poisoning water is bad enough, but depleting the supply is suicidal. The majority of the earth's water is now used to support animal agriculture, and much of it cannot be reclaimed.

About 50% of the water pollution is linked to livestock. Pesticides and fertilizers used in helping grow feed grains run off into lakes and rivers. They also pollute ground water. In the feedlots and stockyard holding pens, there is also a tremendous amount of pesticide runoff. Organic contaminants from huge concentrations of animal excrement and urine at feedlots and stockyards also pollute water. This waste is anywhere from ten to hundreds of times more concentrated than raw domestic sewage. According to a German documentary film (*Fleisch Frisst Menschen* [*Flesh Devours Man*] by Wolfgang Kharuna), nitrates evaporating from open tanks of concentrated livestock waste in the Netherlands have resulted in extremely high levels of forest-killing acid rain.

Feeding the average meat-eater requires about 4,200 gallons of water per day, versus 1,200 gallons per day for a person following a lacto-vegetarian diet. While it takes only 25 gallons of water to produce a pound of wheat, it takes 2,500 gallons of water to produce a pound of meat.

The animals raised for food in the US alone produce 130 times the excrement of the entire human population on Earth, at a rate of 86,600 pounds per second. Only a sixth of this excrement is used as fertilizer; the rest is just dumped into lakes and rivers, untreated. Slaughterhouse runoff is killing millions of fish, and is the main reason why 35% of Earth's rivers and streams are "impaired". In countries with concentrated animal agriculture, the waterways have become rife with a bacteria called pfiesteria. In addition to killing fish, pfiesteria causes open sores, nausea, memory loss, fatigue and disorientation in humans. Even groundwater, which takes thousands of years to restore, is being contaminated. For example, the aquifer under the San Bernadino Dairy Preserve in southern California contains more nitrates and other pollutants than water coming from sewage treatment plants.

But it's not only fresh water sources that are at risk; ocean waters are also imperiled. Dead zones, vast stretches of coastal waters in which nothing can live, are created by untreated hormone, nitrate and antibiotic laden slaughterhouse waste seeping into the soil, groundwater and rivers before contaminating the ocean. According to the EPA, In USA, 35,000 miles of rivers in 22 states and groundwater in 17 states has been permanently contaminated by industrial farm waste.

One pig factory farm produces raw waste equivalent to that of a city of 120000 people -- except unlike a city, it doesn't have a waste treatment facility. Its raw wastes are dumped straight into surrounding rivers and lakes.

New Fatal Diseases

Many of the worst human diseases — BSE, TB, avian flu, West Nile virus, bluetongue, swine flu and now monkey malaria— all are associated with animals of modern meat industry which are kept in crammed, unhygienic conditions in unnaturally large numbers.

Factory Farming - Highest Carbon Footprints

According to a 2006 UN-sponsored report titled "Livestock's Long Shadow," animal factory farming plays a major role in every aspect of environmental collapse, from ozone depletion to ocean dead zones.

If your energy is all engaged in manufacturing tires and wheels, then who will go to the... Actually I have seen in your country. Now the farmers' son, they do not like to remain in the farm. They go in the city. I have seen it. The farmers' son, they do not like to take up the profession of his father. So gradually farming will be reduced, and the city residents, they are satisfied if they can eat meat. And the farmer means keeping the, raising the cattle and killing them, send to the city, and they will think that "We are eating. What is the use of going to..." But these rascals have no brain that "If there is no food grain or grass, how these cattle will be...?" Actually it is happening. They are eating swiftly.
-Srila Prabhupada (Room Conversation with Dr. Theodore Kneupper — November 6, 1976, Vrndavana)

Factory farms, which hold tens of thousands of animals per facility in windowless warehouses, are responsible for more than 18 percent of greenhouse gas emissions worldwide. Emissions from industrial farming are not just caused by cow burps. They are also caused by the one billion tons of waste (including 64 percent of ammonia emissions, the primary producer of acid rain) produced by suffering animals held in extreme confinement.

Containing high levels of hormones and pesticides, this untreated toxic waste is converted into concentrated liquid sewage, known as "slurry." Stored in vast 25-million-gallon lagoons, this endlessly increasing waste releases gases into the atmosphere before some of it gets used to fertilize feed crops. The leading cause of soil and groundwater contamination, lagoon breaches and fertilizer spills are increasingly common.

Even as these animal farms produce more emissions than general transportation, they are also responsible for a majority of emissions produced by all their transportation functions. Most food animals travel thousands of miles in their lifetimes as they are transported between various operations such as stockyards and slaughterhouses. Maintaining the support industries of factory farming also takes a toll on local environments. Planting, fertilizing, irrigating and harvesting feed crops, continually pumping water and sewage, running packing plants and slaughterhouses, all rely on heavy machinery and fossil fuel consumption.

Massive Energy Requirements

Raising animals for food requires more than one-third of all raw materials and fossil fuels used in the United States. Producing a single hamburger patty uses enough fossil fuels to drive a car 20 miles.

Meat production requires 10-20 times more energy per edible tonne than grain production.

> *In an underdeveloped country, don't drink the water; in a developed country, don't breathe the air.*
> *- Changing Times magazine*

Land Usage, Meat and War

A study published in "Plant Foods for Human Nutrition" reveals that an acre of beans or peas produces ten times more protein than an acre of pasture set aside for meat production.

Economic facts like this were known to the ancient Greeks. In Plato's *Republic,* the great Greek philosopher Socrates recommended a vegetarian diet because it would allow a country to make the most intelligent use of its agricultural resources. He warned that if people began eating animals, there would be need for more pasturing land. "And the country which was enough to support the original inhabitants will be too small now, and not enough?", he asked of Glaucon, who replied that this was indeed true "And so we shall go to war, Glaucon, shall we not?" To which Glaucon replied, "Most certainly."

Health and Animal Killing

The human body cannot deal with excessive animal fats in the diet. As early as 1961, the Journal of the American Medical Association stated that ninety to ninety-seven percent of heart disease, the cause of more than half of the deaths in the United States, could be prevented by a vegetarian diet.

Many studies have established the relationship between colon cancer and meat eating. One reason for the incidence of cancer is the high-fat, low-fiber content of the meat-centred diet. The result is a slow transit time through the colon, allowing toxic wastes to do their damage. Meat, while being digested, is known to generate steroid metabolites possessing carcinogenic properties.

Chemicals and Diseases in Meat

Numerous potentially hazardous chemicals, of which consumers are generally unaware, are present in meat and meat products. In

For 200 years we've been conquering Nature. Now we're beating it to death. - Tom McMillan

19

their book, "Poisons In Your Body", Garry and Steven Null give an inside look at the production techniques used by corporately owned animal producers, "The animals are kept alive and fattened by continuous administration of tranquillisers, hormones, antibiotics and 2,700 other drugs," they write, "the process starts even before birth and continues long after death. Although these drugs will still be present in the meat when you eat it, the law does not require that they be listed on the package."

Because of the filthy, overcrowded conditions forced upon animals by the livestock industry, vast amounts of antibiotics must be used, but such rampant use of antibiotics naturally creates antibiotic-resistant bacteria that are passed on to those who eat the meat. The US FDA estimate that penicillin and tetracycline save the meat industry $1.9 billion a year giving them sufficient reason to overlook the potential health hazards. In addition to dangerous chemicals, meat often carries diseases from the animals themselves.

Crammed together in unclean conditions, force-fed and inhumanely treated, animals destined for slaughter contact many more diseases than they ordinarily would. Meat inspectors attempt to filter out unacceptable meats, but because of pressures from industry and lack of sufficient time for examination, much of what passes is far less wholesome than the meat purchaser realizes.

In U.S.A. also, there are so much land vacant. They're not utilizing... Whatever production, they... Sometimes they throw it in the water. And, I, I have heard in this Geneva, that there was excess of milk production. Therefore they want to kill twenty-thousand cows to reduce the milk production. This is their brain. Actually, there is no brain. So they, for brain, they should come to these sastras. They should take guidance. Produce. Produce, utilize. But they'll not utilize. Rather, the limited number of people... At least in India, all the villagers, they have been drawn in the city for producing bolts and nuts. Now eat bolts and nuts.
~Srila Prabhupada (Lecture at World Health Organization, Geneva, June 6, 1974)

Increasing Animal Killings - Decreasing Survival Possibilities

Despite these horrifying statistics, global production of meat is projected to double in the next 10 years.

Average American is already consuming more than 200 pounds of meat per year and rest of the world is trying to follow in their footsteps. In an immediate sense, adopting a meat-free diet may be the most rewarding and effective step an individual can take to help save the planet.

Viewing animals as commodities has had a profoundly negative impact on understanding the world we live in. There is no more important task at hand than combating the false notion that the entire natural world is economically quantifiable or exists simply for our purposes alone.

An animal, an ocean, a forest, a species...and humanity are not separate, but intimately connected in every way. The world consumes 240 billion kilos of meat each year. But more than 75 per cent of what is fed to an animal is lost through metabolism or inedible parts such as bones.

Bleak Future For Humanity

The UN and OIE estimate that in coming decades there will be billions of additional consumers in developing countries eating meat which is factory farmed in developing countries, but currently only about 40 out of the around 200 countries in the world have the capacity to adequately respond to a health crisis originating from animal disease (such as avian flu, West Nile virus, bluetongue, and foot and mouth disease).

Widespread use of antibiotics increases the chance of a pandemic resistant to known measures, which is exacerbated by a globally distributed food system. Decreased genetic diversity increases the chance of a food crisis.

Many people may gladly recycle paper and aluminum cans or take the subway rather than drive to work, they get home and cook up a steak for dinner, unaware that the environmental damage caused to produce that steak far outweighs their other environmental efforts.

We have to make our choice now.... steak on our platter or our very survival.

Cow Represents Earth And Life

There are still parts of the world where people live a pre-industrial life. For example Indonesian Borneo. Daily life in Borneo's upcountry is usually pleasantly dull, as chickens scratch around, the women fan rice on mats to dry it, thunderstorms roll through, the sun dries the muddy paths, flowers riot into bloom, and it all starts over again the next day. Pastoral Mongolia partially fits the category too, with its world revolving around camels, cows and sheep rather than rice and bananas.

Preindustrial life was easy on resources - both human and natural. Before capitalism, most people did not work very long hours. The tempo of life was slow, even leisurely; the pace of work relaxed. People were at peace and so was Earth's environment.

As we have seen in earlier pages, in a vast number of ways and places, the biosphere of this planet is undergoing a great deal of damage. Parts of the environment have already been rendered uninhabitable through toxic wastes and nuclear power plant disasters, while systemic pollution, ozone holes, global warming, and other disasters are increasingly tearing the fabric on which all life depends. That such damage is wrought overwhelmingly by corporations in a competitive international market economy has never been clearer, while the need to replace the existing society with one such as social ecology advances has never been more urgent.

Modernization, the replacement of machines for muscle, is a universal social solvent. Even when resisted by traditional leaders, modernization erodes established social, economic patterns, and threatens ecosystems.

Peasants and tribal members ultimately succumb to mechanisms yielding enhanced productivity. They rapidly scrap traditional practices in favor of those more materially productive.

This modernization has taken a toll on our connection with nature and general web of life. We, like all other life forms, are products of our environment. Its arrogance and ignorance to think that we can survive in isolation. The delicate web of life can not be disturbed without endangering the human survival itself.

Any one with an intact brain would admit the obvious and commonplace fact that animals play a conspicuous part in the life of man. Animals affect everyone's life, whether you're an animal-lover, animal-hater, animal-eater or animal-saver.

Every traditional economy was based on its animals and land. That way the human civilization survived for thousands of years. But in just last one hundred years, everything has been messed up. Survival of humanity and planet itself has come into question. Some one rightly put it, "In the end, cockroaches would prove to be more intelligent than humans if humans destroy themselves. Intelligence is really a survival skill for the entire species and that which survives proves intelligent on a species level."

"It is easier to denature plutonium than to denature the evil spirit of man." ~Albert Einstein

Gaia - The Earthly Deity

Gaia is the primal Greek goddess personifying the Earth. Gaia is a primordial deity in the ancient Greek pantheon and considered a Mother Goddess.

Etymologically Gaia is a compound word of two elements. Ge, meaning "Earth" and 'aia' is a derivative of an Indo-European stem meaning "Grandmother".

This epical name was revived in 1979 by James Lovelock, in 'Gaia: A New Look at Life on Earth' which proposed a Gaia hypothesis. The hypothesis proposes that living organisms and inorganic material are part of a dynamic system that shapes the Earth's biosphere, and maintains the Earth as a fit environment for life. In some Gaia theory approaches, the Earth itself is viewed as an organism with self-regulatory functions. Further books by Lovelock and others popularized the Gaia Hypothesis, which was widely embraced and passed into common usage as part of the heightened awareness of environmental concerns of the 1990s.

Gaia has been widely held throughout history and has been the basis of a belief which still coexists with the great religions. Today the very word 'Gaia' has come to mean ecology and sustainability. There is a thriving green community which runs the portal Gaia.com.

Interestingly, Vedic literatures have similar words, 'Gau' or 'Gava'. The word Gaia has been derived from these words. If we go to Nirukta, the earliest book of etymology from India, and look up its meaning, the two primary meanings of the word 'gau', from which 'gava' is derived, are given in the following order:

1.The planet earth
2.The animal cow.

By using interchangeable words for cow and Earth, Vedas, the oldest repository of knowledge, emphatically state that cow is a representation of the planet earth itself. In almost all Indian languages, cow is knows as 'gai'.

The cow is a complete ecology, a gentle creature and a symbol of abundance. The cow represents life and the sustenance of life. It is so giving, taking nothing but grass. For thousands of years, mankind lived happily, depending on land and cows. To live with cows is to live in perfect cooperation with nature. In a society if you only had cows and agricultural pursuits, you wouldn't require anything else in the name of artificial luxuries.

Cow Protection - The Bottom Line In Sustainable Living

Knowing something of the current state of the environmental movements, we can say with amazing certainty that cow protection and ox power are the very epitome of the bottom line in sustainability. No matter how we look at the topic, there is nothing that comes as close to solving all the problems of the modern world as do cow protection and ox power. Just name an issue of the day: air and water pollution, crime, poverty, unemployment, war, famine, hunger, disease, pestilence, floods, earthquakes, over grazing, global warming, deforestation, etc. A society based on the Vedic principles of cow protection and ox power knows none of these issues. Rama-rajya, or government by Lord Ramachandra, defines a society which is happy

"The sun, the moon and the stars would have disappeared long ago... had they happened to be within the reach of predatory human hands." -Havelock Ellis

in all respects and where there exists perfect harmony between man, nature and other life forms. This is a society wherein no one even suffers from physical ailments or mental agony. In this society, the demigods or the controlling deities of nature are pleased to adjust universal affairs for the complete satisfaction of all the inhabitants, including even those lower than humans (the animals, birds, plants, fish, reptiles, and germs). And cow protection forms the backbone of such an ideal society. *(Sriman Vaninatha dasa)*

Cow & Environmental Protection

Vedic culture's concern for nature and life in general is reflected in an attitude of reverence for the cow. Cow represents the Vedic values of selfless service, strength, dignity, and non-violence. For these reasons, although not all Hindus are vegetarian, they traditionally abstain from eating beef.

Vedic seers could see into the future... to our time when we would feed cows ground up cows and make mad cow disease... a time when mankind would be all bad... they saw us abusing everything...from our fellow creatures to nature all around us.

Africans for thousands of years used cow dung cakes as fuel. In 18th and 19th century missionaries taught them to give up this 'uncivilized' practice. People turned to forests for fuel and in no time the continent was bald.

The cow dung is an important source of producing non-conventional

The bull is the emblem of the moral principle, and the cow is the representative of the earth. When the bull and the cow are in a joyful mood, it is to be understood that the people of the world are also in a joyful mood. The reason is that the bull helps production of grains in the agricultural field, and the cow delivers milk, the miracle of aggregate food values. The human society, therefore, maintains these two important animals very carefully so that they can wander everywhere in cheerfulness. But at the present moment in this age of Kali both the bull and the cow are now being slaughtered and eaten up as foodstuff by a class of men who do not know the brahminical culture.
-Srila Prabhupada (Srimad Bhagavatam 1.16.18)

energy. It is a substitute for firewood and electricity. As a result, the forests can be conserved and their faunal wealth can be enriched.

Every single aspect of cow protection interweaves with protection of our environment. In fact, care for cow represents care for life and nature in general. The cow is central to our life and bio-diversity. Cow protection has a great potential in poverty alleviation and employment generation. It deserves full support at all levels.

Cow Slaughter, Catastrophes And Earthquakes - An Interrelationship

The universe operates under the law of cause and effect. Every action involves and results in a reaction. In Vedic terminology, this is called law of karma. Put in simple words, law of karma is all about reaping what you sow. Life evens out. We have to pay for our deeds.

Law of Karma has had quite a karma. Long after India's seers immortalized it in the Vedas, it suffered bad press under European missionaries who belittled it as "fate" and "fatalism," and today finds itself again in the ascendancy as the subtle and all-encompassing principle which governs man's experiential universe in a way likened to gravity's governance over the physical plane. Like gravity, karma was always there in its fullest potency, even when people did not comprehend it.

Each of us as individuals, as well as each group and nation, is continually creating karma, both good and bad. All thoughts, words, or actions will sooner or later come full circle and return home to

their creators. This is the universal Law of Cause and Effect, which is operating all the time, just like gravity, whether we choose to believe it or not.

"What goes around, comes around" is a statement of fact. An African tribe puts this in a colorful way: "He who excretes on the road, meets flies on his return."

Karma plays a leading role in the world's drift toward environmental catastrophe, and a large part of this karma is generated by unnecessary killing of animals.

Srila Prabhupada states, "We simply request, "Don't kill. Don't maintain slaughterhouses." That is very sinful. It brings a very awkward karmic reaction upon society. Stop these slaughterhouses. We don't say, "Stop eating meat." You can eat meat, but don't take it from the slaughterhouse, by killing. Simply wait and you'll get the carcasses."

Cow Slaughter And Earthquakes

Physicists M M Bajaj, Ibrahim and Vijayraj Singh have proposed the theory that animal slaughter and natural calamities like earthquakes have an interrelationship and research papers on this theory have been presented in many international conferences. The theory presents the hypothesis of large-scale abattoir activity as the causative agent for major earthquakes.

They put forward a forceful plea to stop slaughter of animals, birds, and fish with special reference to cows. Their theory makes an interesting reading because science still does not have proper answers as to why the earthquakes happen and how they can be predicted with reasonable accuracy. This theory is being hailed for filling the gaps in the science of seismology, still a nascent science.

The theory, with the help of highly technical and scientific jargon, attempts to explain that butchering of animals in the abattoirs worldwide has something to do with the quakes. The theory examines the complex role of nociceptive waves (or the waves generated by the animals on the verge of being butchered) in shear-wave splitting which is related to seismic anisotropy. This splitting is associated with the cracks in the crust aligned by stress. The origin of earthquakes due to the interaction of nociception waves with gravity waves is critically examined in the theory. An earthquake of 8 Richter occurs only when the resonant frequency is extremely high. Low frequency resonances lead to earthquakes of 0.1 to 0.2 Richter. Low frequency resonances are hardly felt or realised by the ordinary people. High frequency resonances (originating from the slaughter of millions of animals daily for years together) lead to powerful singularities with the gravity waves. In this way the theory proposes that shear wave splitting mainly occurs due to aligned fluid-filled inclusions and abattoir activity.

Dying Animals Cause Acoustic Anisotropy

Authors make a point that acoustic anisotropy leads to a very strong anisotropic stress on a rock. The daily butchering of thousands of animals continually for several years generates acoustic anisotropy due to Einsteinian Pain Waves (EPW) emitted by dying animals. And the accumulated acoustic anisotropy is found to be related with the stress history of rocks. Nociception waves interact with the earth's natural rhythmatic vibrations and lead to responses which are extremely powerful (of the order of 10 40 MW) causing crack density (CD) which is directly proportional to EPW. Also the factor of tectonic plate movement has been taken into account. The Einsteinian Pain Waves are responsible for the release of Radon in the ground. The increase of Radon concentration in the groundwater and its relationship with the earthquakes is said to have been experimentally

If one gives another living entity unnecessary pain, one will certainly be punished by the laws of nature with a similar pain. Although the hunter Mrgari was uncivilized, he still had to suffer the results of his sinful activities. However, if a civilized man kills animals regularly in a slaughterhouse to maintain his so-called civilization, using scientific methods and machines to kill animals, one cannot even estimate the suffering awaiting him. So-called civilized people consider themselves very advanced in education, but they do not know about the stringent laws of nature. According to nature's law, it is a life for a life. We can hardly imagine the sufferings of one who maintains a slaughterhouse.
-Srila Prabhupada (Chaitanya Charitamrta, Madhya 24.249)

verified by several Chinese and Japanese scientists. Fault lines of the earth provide the most convenient place for the release of pressure induced by the geomorphological process and triggered by LSFAOß (living state forced annihilation operator of beta type). *BIS effect* of type II is able to trigger the seismic episodes of 6 to 7 Richter.

The theory claims that since the EPW travel a great distance with time, abattoirs of one location may lead to havoc in another geographical area. Theory proposes closing down of all the abattoirs in the world. This theory is a 600 page work and its hypotheses make liberal use of complex mathematical and statistical formulas.

The theory also explores the possibility of earthquake prediction based on well defined principles. Theory may present answers to the question as to why experts have so much trouble in predicting earthquakes.

This subject has originated from the **B**ajaj-**I**brahim-**S**ingh effect or BIS effect and it was first presented in Suzdal (Russia) in 1995. Since then some scholars have written chapters on Bisology in their books, an Indian Journal has brought out a special issue devoted to the subject and several scholars have studied this subject in their Ph.D theses submitted to different universities around the world.

Stop Killing The Cows, Stop Killing The Planet

We can safely conclude that reducing or eliminating meat consumption would have substantial positive effects on the environment. Fewer trees would be cut, less soil would be eroded, and desertification would be substantially slowed. A major source of air and water pollution would be removed, and scarce fresh water would be conserved. "To go beyond beef is to transform our very

We simply request, "Don't kill. Don't maintain slaughterhouses." That is very sinful. It brings down very severe karmic reactions upon society. Stop these slaughterhouses. We don't say, "Stop eating meat." You can eat meat, but don't take it from the slaughterhouse, by killing. Simply wait, and you'll get the carcasses.
~*Srila Prabhupada (Journey of Self Discovery 6.5: Slaughterhouse Civilization)*

thinking about appropriate behavior toward nature," says Jeremy Rifkin. "We come to appreciate the source of our sustenance, the divinely inspired creation that deserves nurture and requires stewardship. Nature is no longer viewed as an enemy to be subdued and tamed."

Waste not the smallest thing created, for grains of sand make mountains, and atomies infinity.
~E. Knight

2.

Cow
An Engine Of Progress And Prosperity

In last several decades, world economy has been globalized and its not the best thing to have happened to our finances. The economic system built on a need for constant growth obviously can't last long in a finite world. Small is beautiful...and sustainable. There are limits to growth and the world economy has crossed these limits.

The history is trying to repeat itself in last two years. Headlines are blaring - Financial markets in a free-fall, Chaos on Wall St., International markets in a tailspin, European bailout, More banks to fail, Investors shy away amidst growing fears, Congress approves bailout, 51 Million to loose jobs, China goes down in first quarter etc.

These foreboding headlines are indications of something coming out way, if we are willing to listen. Global Financial system is increasingly proving to be a farce and it has become exponentially more so as Treasury/Federal Reserve bailouts in the financial sector become the rule rather than the exception.

America's unquenchable materialistic appetite is the machine that fuels a global economy. Japan's economy would collapse if it were not for the billions of dollars per year gained in trading with America. When America goes into a recession, the world follows. When America's economy is doing fine, so does the world's.

War - A Fall out of Economic Collapse

An economic collapse is a devastating breakdown of a national, regional, or territorial economy. It is essentially a severe economic depression characterised by a sharp increase in bankruptcy and unemployment. A full or near-full economic collapse is often quickly followed by months, years, or even decades of economic depression, social chaos, and civil unrest. Such crises have both been seen to afflict capitalist market economies and state controlled economies.

Today it feels like the summer of 1931. The world's biggest financial institutions have had a heart attack. The global currency system is breaking down. The policy doctrines that got us into this mess are bankrupt. No world leader seems able to discern the problem, let alone forge a solution. The International Monetary Fund has abdicated into schizophrenia. All these does not forebode well for an already unstable world

Historically, the causes for war have always been economic in nature, no matter what the official reasons were. Economic disintegration and war go hand in hand, as both have a similar, imperial root.

If world economies continue to disintegrate and fall apart, war would be a real threat. History is a witness that bucks have been the basis of the great wars. Two world wars were fought to counteract British colonialism and their financial exploitation of the whole world. Hitler termed the British as a 'shopkeepers' nation. The Germans made better

So actually, human opulence means not these tin cars. Once it is dashed with another car, it is finished, no value. Human opulence means the society must have enough gold, enough jewelry, enough silk, enough grains, enough milk, enough vegetables, like that. That is opulent. That is opulence. Formerly a person was considered rich by two things: dhanyena dhanavan. How much grain stock he has got at his home. A big, big barn, filled with grains. Still in India, if I am going to give my daughter to some family, to see the family's opulence, I go to see the house, and if I see there are many, many barns' stock of grains and many cows, then it is very good.
-Srila Prabhupada (Srimad-Bhagavatam 1.9.2 — Los Angeles, May 16, 1973)

and cheaper products but all the world markets were occupied by the British. This led to the World War II.

Modern word for unscrupulous colonials is corporations. Corporatisation is the modern way of colonizing the world. Today's world is getting ground under the corporate jackboot. These huge corporations make obscene profits out of human misery and they want the world to remain in misery. They run our health care industry. They run our oil and gas companies. They run our bloated weapons industry. They run Wall Street and the major investment firms. They run our manufacturing firms. They also, ominously, run our government. World is simply not a safe place in the shadows of these greedy monsters. They want profits - when economy thrives and they want profits - when economy dies. Profits in a dying economy means war. That's the only way to go about it

Simple And Healthy Economics

By Srila Prabhupada

Money is required for purchasing food, but the animals, they do not know that food can be purchased. They are searching after food. But we are civilized; we are searching after money. Money is required

Ample food grains can be produced through agricultural enterprises, and profuse supplies of milk, yogurt and ghee can be arranged through cow protection. Abundant honey can be obtained if the forests are protected. Unfortunately, in modern civilization, men are busy killing the cows that are the source of yogurt, milk and ghee, they are cutting down all the trees that supply honey, and they are opening factories to manufacture nuts, bolts, automobiles and wine instead of engaging in agriculture. How can the people be happy? They must suffer from all the misery of materialism. Their bodies become wrinkled and gradually deteriorate until they become almost like dwarves, and a bad odor emanates from their bodies because of unclean perspiration resulting from eating all kinds of nasty things. This is not human civilization. If people actually want happiness in this life and want to prepare for the best in the next life, they must adopt a Vedic civilization.
-Srila Prabhupada (Srimad Bhagavatam 5.16.25)

for purchasing food. Why don't you produce food directly? That is intelligence. You are getting money, very good. What is that money? A paper. You are being cheated. It is written there, "hundred dollars." But what is that hundred dollars? It is a piece of paper only. But because we are so foolish, we are accepting a piece of paper, hundred dollars, and the struggle for existence for a piece of paper. Why don't you be intelligent — "Why shall I take the piece of paper? Give me food"? But that intelligence you have lost. Therefore my Guru

Maharaja used to say the present human society is combination of cheaters and cheated, that's all. No intelligent person. Formerly money was gold and silver coins. It had some value. But what is the present currency? Simply piece of paper. Bunch of papers. During the last war the government failed in Germany, and these bunch of papers were thrown in the street. Nobody was caring. Nobody was caring.

So our civilization is based on that way. You require food. That's fact. Therefore Krsna says, *annad bhavanti bhutani* [Bg. 3.14]. You produce your food. Anywhere you can produce your food. There is enough land. In Australia you have got enough land. In Africa you have enough land, uncultivated. No. They'll not produce food. They will produce coffee and tea and slaughter animals. This is their business. I understand that in your country animals are slaughtered and exported for trade. Why export? You produce your own food and be satisfied. Why you are after that piece of hundred dollars paper? Produce your own food and eat sumptuously, be healthy and chant Hare Krsna. This is civilization. This is civilization. *(Lecture, Bhagavad-gita 9.4 — Melbourne, April 22, 1976)*

Living Cows - Better Than Dead Ones

A man and his wife owned a very special goose. Every day the goose would lay a golden egg, which made the couple very rich. "Just think," said the man's wife, "If we could have all the golden eggs that are inside the goose, we could be richer much faster." "You're right," said her husband, "We wouldn't have to wait for the goose to lay her egg every day."

India's civilization was based on village residence. They would live very peacefully in the villages. In the evening there would be bhagavata-katha. They will hear. That was Indian culture. They had no artificial way of living, drinking tea, and meat-eating and wine and illicit sex. No. Everyone was religious and satisfied by hearing -- what we are just introducing -- Bhagavatam, Bhagavad-gita, Puranas, and live simple life, keeping cows, village life as it is exhibited by Krsna, Vrndavana
-Srila Prabhupada (Morning Walk -- Durban, October 13, 1975)

So, the couple killed the goose and cut her open, only to find that she was just like any other goose. She had no golden eggs inside of her at all, and they had no more golden eggs.

This is among the best known of Aesop's Fables and use of the phrase has become idiomatic of an unprofitable action motivated by greed.

Cow killing bears resemblance to the man's folly in the story. We are slaughtering cows to get beef. But cows can give much more daily. It is our obstinacy or ignorance of her contributions that makes us kill and eat her.

In 1971 Stewart Odend'hal of the University of Missouri conducted a detailed study of cows in Bengal and found that far from depriving humans of food, they ate only inedible remains of harvested crops (rice hulls, tops of sugarcane, etc.) and grass. "Basically", he said, "the cattle convert items of little direct human value into products of immediate utility." This should put to rest the myth that people are starving in India because they will not kill their cows. Interestingly enough, India seems to have surmounted her food problems, which have always had more to do with occasional severe drought or political upheaval than with sacred cows. A panel of experts at the Agency for International Development, in a statement cited in the United States Congressional Record for December 2nd 1980, concluded "India produces enough to feed all its people."

If allowed to live, cows produce High quality, protein rich foods in amounts that stagger the imagination. It is abundantly clear that cows (living ones) are one of mankind's most valuable food resources.

Life Line of A Nation

India has thirty percent of the world's cattle and there are twenty six breeds. The cow is a symbol of wealth and abundance and has a place everywhere in India. Cows can be seen wandering along the city streets and country sides, on posters and carved from wood and

"I don't care how many pails of milk I lose, as long as I don't lose the cow"
- Russian Proverb

stone. They are allowed to roam freely and subsist on garbage or grass along the roadside. Of course all this is changing now and apathy towards cows is growing.

Cow slaughter is banned in India except in two states, West Bengal and Kerala. Cows are regularly shipped to these two states for slaughter even though it is illegal to transport them across borders. Cow transport in India is extremely cruel and many get injured and die in the process. For days and weeks together, cows and bulls travel in trucks or railway wagons, crammed and without food or water. This sort of treatment to a gentle and innocent animal is the last frontier of inhumanity.

Cow products like milk, yogurt, ghee, buttermilk and cheese are indispensable ingredients in Indian cuisine. Indian kitchens require liberal stock of these valuable products on day to day basis. Male calves are highly valued by Indian farmers unlike in West where they are slaughtered at a very young age. Male calves as oxen form the backbone of Indian agriculture and rural transport. In post harvest operations, they stomp through mounds of cut wheat and rice. A farmer's loss of cattle can affect his livelihood and when a cow dies she is mourned like a family member.

One living cow gives in a year 230 kg. of methane gas, organic fertilizers for 3-4 acres land and 600-3000 liters of milk. But unfortunately every day in India over a hundred thousand cows are killed now.

Traditionally in India, cow was reared mainly for her urine and manure. Milk was considered a byproduct. As the science of utilizing these products was lost, cow's utility came to be confined to her milk. As a result, as soon as she goes dry, she is a burden and ends up in a slaughter house. Fortunately, India is seeing a revival of cow

The economic development requires cow protections, but these rascals do not know. Their economic development is cow killing. Just see, rascal civilization. Don't be sorry. It is sastra. Don't think that I am criticizing the Western civilization. It is sastra says. Very experienced.
-Srila Prabhupada (Lecture, Srimad-Bhagavatam 5.5.3 -- Stockholm, September 9, 1973)

product manufacturing. In various cow shelters and villages across the country, dozens of products are being produced from cow urine and dung. Products like medicines, fertilizers, pesticides, soaps, toothpowder, paper, tiles, coils, incense, phenyl, hand wash, glass cleaner etc. are becoming popular. If this aspect of cow economics is rightly promoted, the Indian villages once again can become prosperous. Chemical fertilizers and pesticides are wreaking havoc on agriculture and thousands of farmers are committing suicide every year.

India's 'Development' - An Evaluation

Since post independence liberalisation of the economy, India has been blindly imitating the Western economic model (especially in

Dhanyena dhanavan. If you have got grain, then you are rich. And if you have got cows, then you are rich. This is the standard of Vedic richness. Dhanyena dhanavan gavayo dhanavan. They don't say, "Keep some papers and you become rich." All rascal, one thousand dollar I promise to pay, a piece of paper. Practical, we have got enough food grains. We have got enough... That is richness. What is use of paper? Even gold you have got, you have to exchange. And if you have grain, immediate food. Just boil with milk, and it is nectarean, param anna, immediately. Take some wood collected from the woods and have fire, put the milk and the grains-oh, you'll get so nice food, nutritious, full of vitamin, and so easily made. It is practical. So tasteful, so nutritious, and don't require. If you simply boil little milk and little grain, whole day, so much sweet rice, you take. You don't require any more. And if you add little apples and fruits, oh, it is heavenly. Your whole day free from any food anxiety, and you can work. And you can work. You can chant Hare Krsna. Make this ideal life here. America has got good potency. We have got so much land here. We can have hundreds of New Vrindabans or farms like that. And people will be happy. And invite all the world, "Please come and live with us. Why you are suffering congestion, overpopulation? Welcome here.
-Srila Prabhupada (Room Conversation — June 28, 1976, New Vrindaban)

*In Vrindavan, the cows, the bulls and the calves were thoroughly
smeared with a mixture of turmeric and oil, mixed with varieties
of minerals. Their heads were bedecked with peacock feathers,
and they were garlanded and covered with cloth and golden
ornaments. (Srimad Bhagavatam 10.5.7)*

terms of opening slaughterhouses). Local conditions have been
completely ignored. Anything indigenous or traditional is considered
crap. Leaders are living in a 'made in London' dream world. As a
result the benefit of economic growth has been cornered by a small
minority. This minority lives lavishly while the vast majority continues
to rot in abject poverty and deprivation.

According to Forbes, the number of billionaires in India doubled
to 52 in 2009, their combined net worth reached $ 276 billion or a
quarter of the country's GDP.

The National Commission for Enterprises in Unorganised Sector
(NCEUS), chaired by Arjun Sengupta, has found that 836 million
Indians are poor and vulnerable, living on less than Rs 20 (40 cents)
per day and have hardly experienced any improvement in their living
standard since the early 1990s.

What can Rs 20 possibly fetch? For 836 million Indians, Rs 20 per
day, or Rs 600 a month, buys them their daily sustenance.

Technically, a large chunk of these 836 million Indians 77 per cent
of the country's population are above the poverty line at Rs 12 (25
cents) per day.

Published in 2007, this was the first authoritative study on the state of informal or unorganised employment in India, compiled by the National Commission for Enterprises in the Unorganised Sector (NCEUS), a government-affiliated body.

Shameless Planning Commissions

In September 2011, in an affidavit before the Supreme Court the Planning Commission said that an individual income of just Rs. 25 (50 cents) a day constitutes adequate "private expenditure on food, education and health."

The affidavit bases its assertion on the findings of the Suresh Tendulkar Committee, which pegged the poverty line at Rs. 447 ($10) a month, or about Rs. 15 (30 cents) a day, at 2004-2005 prices.

Experts reacted with dismay to the affidavit. National Advisory Council member Aruna Roy said it reflected the government's lack

of empathy for the poor. "This extremely low estimated expenditure is aimed at artificially reducing the number of persons below the poverty line and thus reduce government expenditure on the poor," she alleged.

The shameless committee said its "proposed poverty lines have been validated by checking the adequacy of actual private expenditure per capita near the poverty lines on food, education and health by comparing them with normative expenditures consistent with nutritional, education and health outcomes."

This is the outcome of the decades of 'development and progress' and scams and squanderings. Shameless 'planning' commission members, living on fat salaries and sitting in plush offices, can hardly be more insensitive and insensible. They have overlooked the fact that trillions are stashed away in foreign accounts and trillions are being wasted in useless games and swallowed in scams while millions starve.

India Needs Cow

Agriculture, the NCEUS report found, was a fertile ground for poverty, especially for small and marginal farmers, 84 per cent of whom spent more than they earned and were often caught in debt traps.

Gandhi wanted it ... Village organization. He started that Wardha Ashram. But you have rejected. What Gandhi can do? That was good proposal -- to remain satisfied in one's own place. That was Gandhi's proposal. That "Don't go to the city, town, for so-called better advantage of life. Remain in your own home, produce your food, and be satisfied there." That was Gandhi's policy. The economic problem he wanted to solve by keeping cows, by agriculture, by spinning thread. "You want food, shelter and cloth? Produce here, and remain here. Don't be allured by the capitalists and go to cities and engage in industries." But Jawaharlal Nehru wanted, overnight, to Americanize the whole India. That is the folly.
-Srila Prabhupada (Room Conversation with Reporter from Researchers Magazine -- July 24, 1973, London)

Reintroduction of cows can drastically change the rural landscape in India but the entire government machinery is geared towards killing and exporting cows. After independence, it took 65 long years for the Indian leaders to realize their cherished dream - to make India a world leader in beef export. This feat was achieved in year 2012 under the able leadership of a cow eating leader. And now finally the founders of modern India can rest in peace. Having realized their dreams, these founders must be reveling in their graves.

Wealth Means Land, Cows and Grains

According to the Vedic Scriptures real wealth means to possess some land, cows and a store of grains. These things are practical. The land and the forests in conjunction with cows and food grains provide all the necessities of life.

Financial adviser Howard Ruff and survivalist Sally Harrington, are more down to earth. In a world spinning toward political, economic,

Formerly even in the villages you would see that a common man has very good stock of foodgrains and cows, dhanvena dhanavan, gavaya dhanavan. Formerly the standard of richness was considered how many morai.. the bank, what is called? Where grain is stocked? Silo. So in India it is called morai, grain stock. And how many cows one has got in stock. Then he is rich man. Nowadays how much paper money he has got. Actually it has no value. Suppose you have got some papers. Each paper it is written there "one thousand dollars." But if there is no grain, what will this one-thousand-dollars paper will do? It actually so happened in the last war in Germany. Their money was thrown in the street. Nobody cared to take it, because it has no exchange. So long the paper money you can exchange, there is value. Otherwise it is paper only. But if you have got actual commodity—grains and cows—then you can eat in any circumstances. Never mind war is going on; you don't care. You get sufficient food. What you will do with the paper money?
- Srila Prabhupada (Lecture on Srimad Bhagavatam 5.5.3, Vrindavan, , October 25, 1976)

and ecological disaster, Ruff explains why grains and beans are at least as good an investment as silver and gold.

"You spend hundreds of dollars every year to insure your cars against the accident you fully expect not to have," says Ruff, "and you can't eat the cancelled checks. Your money is wasted unless you're 'lucky' enough to have an accident. Food storage is the insurance you can eat."

Adds Harrington, "Wheat, if kept dry and protected from rodents and insects, will last for two or three thousand years. Some that was found in King Tut's tomb was still edible, and it even germinated."

The forests provide building materials for dwellings, honey, flowers, fruits and medicinal herbs and drugs. The rivers provide fresh drinking water and are a source of natural fertilizer and gems. By the arrangement of nature the rivers flood the land periodically, thus replacing the lost nutrients in the soil.

If you have grains, fruits and dairy products like milk, cheese, cream, yogurt and butter, you can live happily ever after. Fact is, you can not eat your currency notes or computer chips.

By nature's perfect arrangement, land and cows compliment each other in maintaining the cycle of life. Land supports cow by supplying her feed and she replenishes the land with her manure. When the cow population swells, the soil in the area comes alive. If cows are allowed to graze on waste or barren land, gradually its fertility returns. This is because Goddess of Prosperity resides in cow dung. In India of yesteryears, there were so many happy cows they used to moisten the ground with their milk. Today its their blood that is splattered all over.

When we produce food grains and vegetables, we can give protection to the cows; while giving protection to the cows, we can draw from them abundant quantities of milk; and by getting enough milk and combining it with food grains and vegetables, we can prepare hundreds of nectarean foods. We can happily eat this food and thus avoid industrial enterprises and joblessness.
~Srila Prabhupada (Srimad Bhagavatam 8.6.12)

44

Currency Notes, Share Certificates - Bunch of Papers

Magic of Modern Economy - From Prince To Pauper In Minutes

Story of 1929 Wall street crash was repeated in India on 21st January 2008. On a day, known as Black Monday, investors lost Rs 6 trillion within minutes of the Indian stock exchange's opening in Mumbai. The authorities immediately suspended the trading for one hour. The sensex tumbled 2,029 points within minutes of the start of trading.

This loss of Rs 6,54,887 crore came on top of over Rs 11 trillion loss suffered by investors at Dalal Street in the last six days. Small investors were advised to stay away from the markets. Investors' wealth - measured in terms of cumulative market capitalisation of all the listed companies - declined by a whopping Rs 18,40,173 crore.

As per information available on the Bombay Stock Exchange website, the total market capitalisation stood at Rs 59,53,525 crore at the end of the Black Monday's trading against Rs 71,38,810 crore before the stock exchange began business on January 14. The cause for this was attributed on concerns regarding the US economy going into recession. Many people suffered heart attacks and several committed suicide.

A land and cow based economy is definitely more stable and offers better scope for an anxiety free living. The stress of modern life is responsible for a lifestyle disease pandemic. In preindustrial mode of living, these diseases are unknown.

Apart from the story of January 2008 in India, by October 2008, investors across the world lost more than $10 trillion - an amount more than 10 times of the entire investor wealth in India.

All 52 equity markets of the world suffered a loss of $10.5 trillion in 2008 as per the leading rating agency and financial data provider, Standard and Poors.

"Wheat, if kept dry and protected from rodents and insects, will last for two or three thousand years. Some that was found in King Tut's tomb was still edible, and it even germinated." -Harrington,

Indian stock market valuation nearly halved in 2008. 2009 might offer some relief but situation remains volatile as ever before. For two square meals, mankind is undergoing so much anxiety and frustration. Even animals live far more peacefully though they have no banking, industries or fiscal systems. An elephant requiring 300 kgs of food daily has no anxiety whereas human beings consuming 300 gms daily are dying from anxiety.

Coming back to America's crash of 1929; America was having an economic explosion. Immigrants were pouring in. There were more jobs than people. Farmers were leaving their fields for factories, making twice the income for half the labor. Politicians confidently portrayed a picture of an endless era of unprecedented prosperity. The prophets of gloom and doom were ignored as crazies.

Fall is a beautiful time of year. A time of thanksgiving, a remembrance of God's blessing upon the birth of a Christian country. The leaves are in full bloom, ready to fall. It is a time for Sunday drives through the country without a thought of the oncoming winter. Splashes of color cover the hills and valleys. As the squirrels wisely gather food for a cold long winter, a nation is borrowing and spending because of a thriving economy that can promise only spring and summer.

A ship sails to England in the early part of October 1929, full of wealthy entrepreneurs, a sign of absolute faith in a thriving American economy. While they were on their carefree vacation, enjoying the

Residents of Vrndavana had become highly prosperous simply by protecting cows, since Indra wanted to destroy their so-called pride based on wealth by killing their animals. Well-tended cows produce large quantities of milk, from which come cheese, butter, yogurt, ghee and so on. These foods are delicious by themselves and also enhance other foods, such as fruits, vegetables and grains. Bread and vegetables are delicious with butter, and fruit is especially appetizing when mixed with cream or yogurt. Dairy products are always desirable in civilized society, and the surplus can be traded for many valuable commodities. Thus, simply by a Vedic dairy enterprise, the residents of Vrndavana were wealthy, healthy and happy, even in the material sense
~Srila Prabhupada (Srimad Bhagavatam 10.25.6)

pleasure away from the stress of their jobs, a powerful economic tremor rippled through the United States. On October 24, 1929, 12,000,000 shares of common stocks traded in a single afternoon. By Monday, October 28th, the trading averages had dropped by 20 points. On Tuesday, October 29th, virtually all trades were to sell. It became 'A Nightmare On Wall Street.' Investors became panic–stricken, resulting in a huge economic land slide. AT&T was down a hundred points, General Electric, 90 points and General Motors, plummeted 150 points. Sixteen million shares were traded at a loss of 10 billion dollars. This was equivalent to twice the amount of currency of the entire USA. Headlines proclaimed, Wall Street Crashes. Tens of millions of people's life savings became completely useless. Millionaires were reduced to the unemployed. On Wall Street, it rained the bodies of men jumping from their offices high above. When the ship returned full of happy–go–lucky entrepreneurs, they were worth the clothes on their backs. An economic winter had fallen upon America which would effect the entire earth. An ice age that would last four long years. Full recovery came only after World War II. Life blood of modern economics is war and violence. Nothing invigorates our economic system like a war.

At the close of World War II, many countries did not return to a civilian economy, but kept to a 'permanent war economy.' The term 'permanent war economy' refers to the economic component within the military-industrial complex whereby the collusion between militarism and war profiteering are manifest as a permanently subsidized industry. Today the world retains the character of a global war economy; even in peacetime, with massive military expenditure.

Wars always existed in human society but for thousands of years the methodology of war practically remained the same. It was a part time activity at best.

Paraphernalia of war was produced by decentralised small scale industries but these industries also had practical peacetime applications. For example, industries making swords in times of war could make plowshares in times of peace. It was not until the late 19th to early 20th century that military weaponry became so complex as to require a large subset of industry dedicated solely to its procurement. Firearms, artillery, steamships, and later aircraft and nuclear weapons were markedly different from their ancient predecessors.

These newer, more complex weapons required highly specialized

It is very important to note in this connection how wealthy the inhabitants of Vrndavana were simply by raising cows. All the cowherd men belonged to the vaisya community, and their business was to protect the cows and cultivate crops. By their dress and ornaments, and by their behavior, it appears that although they were in a small village, they still were rich in material possessions. They possessed such an abundance of various kinds of milk products that they were throwing butter lavishly on each other's bodies without restriction. Their wealth was in milk, yogurt, clarified butter and many other milk products, and by trading their agricultural products, they were rich in various kinds of jewelry, ornaments and costly garments. Not only did they possess all these things, but they could give them away in charity lavishly, as did Nanda Maharaja.

-Srila Prabhupada (Krishna Book 5: The Meeting of Nanda and Vasudeva)

labor, knowledge and machinery to produce. The time and supporting industry necessary to construct weapon systems of increasing complexity and massive integration, made it no longer feasible to create assets only in times of war. Instead, nations dedicated portions of their economies for the full time production of war assets. The increasing reliance of military on industry gave rise to a stable partnership—the military–industrial complex.

War and violence and death and destruction lie at the heart of modern economic system. World economies would collapse if the wars are stopped. If you are looking for economics of peace, you have to look somewhere else.

Vrindavan - An Affluent Pastoral Community

India of yesteryears is exemplified by Vrindavan, an ancient pastoral village. Vrindavan is a typical representation of Vedic India, known for her immense wealth and a highly advanced culture. Cows formed its backbone and Indian culture was rightly called 'cow culture'.

When the British colonized India, the Governor Robert Clive made a careful study of India's economic and agricultural systems. He observed how Indian society was firmly rooted in its age-old customs and sound economic and agricultural practices. He was very impressed with the civilizational setup of India.

His mood is reflected in a letter written by Lord MCLau dated February 2, 1835.

"I have traveled across the length and breath of India and I have not seen one person who is a beggar, who is a thief, such

Cow protection is recommended in the Vedic literature because it is giving the most valuable foodstuff, milk. Apart from other sentiments, it is supplying, and in exchange of nothing. She simply eats some grasses from the ground. That's all. You don't have to provide cows with foodstuff. The things which you refuse, you take the grain and you supply the skin. You take the fruit pulp, you supply the skin. You take the, I mean to say, from paddy. You take the rice. You supply the straw and she delivers you a very nice foodstuff.
- Srila Prabhupada (Lecture, Srimad-Bhagavatam 5.5.3 , Boston, May 4, 1968)

wealth I have seen in this country, such high moral values, people of such caliber (of noble character), that I do not think we would ever conquer this country...........unless we break the very backbone of this nation which is her spiritual and cultural heritage."

So during his surveys in 1740, Robert Clive found in Arcot District of Tamil Nadu, 54 Quintals of rice was harvested from one acre of land using cow manure and pesticides. Cow was the foundation of this great nation and cows greatly outnumbered men. He realized that unless this foundation was shaken up, they could not keep their hold on this country for too long. This inspired him to open the first slaughterhouse in India in 1760. This slaughterhouse was capable of processing hundreds of cows every week. Cow slaughter was initiated as a part of the master plan to destabilize India.

Prior to the British, Moghuls ruled India for 800 years. During their rule, cow killing was sporadic. Many Moghul kings like Babar, Akbar and Jahangir banned cow killing. When not banned, number of cows killed in a year never exceeded more than a few thousand. Cow slaughter in India has a British origin.

To this extent, the British were quite successful. Cow slaughter, engineered by them, divided Hindu and Muslim communities which had coexisted peacefully for the last 800 years. Millions died in ensuing riots which lasted for decades. To this day, India and Pakistan are locked in bitter enmity and continually suffering.

Robert Clive started a number of slaughter houses before he left India. By 1910, 350 slaughterhouses were working day and night. India was reduced to severe poverty. Millions were dying from hunger and malnutrition. Age-old cottage industries were devastated and village artisans took up jobs as coolies in cities. Manchester cloth effectively destroyed Indian handlooms enterprise. Using Indian money and men, British were expanding their empire all over the world.

Bereft of its cattle wealth, India had to approach England for industrial manure. Thus industrial manures like urea and phosphate made their way to India. Indian villages, where flowed streams of butter and milk, became haunted hamlets, wretched and starving. A Paradise was lost. An India where horses and bullocks were made to drink ghee, was now suffering from a scarcity of margarine. It was total devastation of a great civilization.

The British established an educational system which decried anything connected with Indian tradition. This was a crafty engineering by Macaulay who said, "We must at present do our best to form a class of persons Indian in blood and colour but English in tastes, in opinion, in morals, and in intellect." He did this so effectively that even after sixty years of independence Indians still continue to exist in a state of stupor, unable (and even unwilling!) to extricate themselves from one of the greatest hypnoses woven over a whole nation.

By the time British departed from India, thousands of slaughterhouses were in operation and now its hard to keep a count. The result - 40000 suicides by Indian farmers every year.

Prosperity and affluence of Vrindavan, a representative Indian village based on cow protection, is immortalized in pages of Srimad Bhagavatam:

Sukadeva Gosvami said: Nanda Maharaja was naturally very magnanimous, and when Lord Sri Krsna appeared as his son, he was overwhelmed by jubilation. Therefore, after bathing and purifying himself and dressing himself properly, he invited brahmanas who knew how to recite Vedic mantras. After having these qualified brahmanas recite auspicious Vedic hymns, he arranged to have the Vedic birth ceremony celebrated for his newborn child according to the rules and regulations, and he also arranged for worship of the demigods and forefathers.

Nanda Maharaja gave numerous cows, completely decorated with cloth and jewels, in charity to the brahmanas. He also gave them seven hills of grain, covered with jewels and with cloth decorated with golden embroidery.

The brahmanas recited auspicious Vedic hymns, which purified the environment by their vibration. The experts in reciting old histories like the Puranas, the experts in reciting the histories of royal families, and general reciters all chanted, while singers sang and many kinds of musical instruments, like bheris and dundubhis, played in accompaniment.

Vrajapura, the residence of Nanda Maharaja, was fully decorated with varieties of festoons and flags, and in different places, gates were made with varieties of flower garlands, pieces of cloth, and mango leaves. The courtyards, the gates near the roads, and everything within the rooms of the houses were perfectly swept and washed with water.

The cows, the bulls and the calves were thoroughly smeared with a mixture of turmeric and oil, mixed with varieties of minerals. Their heads were bedecked with peacock feathers, and they were garlanded and covered with cloth and golden ornaments.

O King Pariksit, the cowherd men dressed very opulently with valuable ornaments and garments such as coats and turbans. Decorated in this way and carrying various presentations in their hands, they approached the house of Nanda Maharaja.

The gopi wives of the cowherd men were very pleased to hear that mother Yasoda had given birth to a son, and they began to decorate themselves very nicely with proper dresses, ornaments, black ointment for the eyes, and so on.

Their lotuslike faces extraordinarily beautiful, being decorated with saffron and newly grown kunkuma, the wives of the cowherd men hurried to the house of mother Yasoda with presentations in their hands. Because of natural beauty, the wives had full hips and full breasts, which moved as they hurried along.

In the ears of the gopis were brilliantly polished jeweled earrings, and from their necks hung metal lockets. Their hands were decorated with bangles, their dresses were of varied colors, and from their hair, flowers fell onto the street like showers. Thus while going to the house of Maharaja Nanda, the gopis, their earrings, breasts and garlands moving, were brilliantly beautiful.

Offering blessings to the newborn child, Krsna, the wives and daughters of the cowherd men said, "May You become the King of Vraja and long maintain all its inhabitants." They sprinkled a mixture of turmeric powder, oil and water upon the birthless Supreme Lord and offered their prayers.

Now that the all-pervading, unlimited Lord Krsna, the master of the cosmic manifestation, had arrived within the estate of Maharaja Nanda, various types of musical instruments resounded to celebrate the great festival.

In gladness, the cowherd men enjoyed the great festival by splashing one another's bodies with a mixture of curd, condensed milk, butter and water. They threw butter on one another and smeared it on one another's bodies.

The great-minded Maharaja Nanda gave clothing, ornaments and cows in charity to the cowherd men in order to please Lord Visnu, and thus he improved the condition of his own son in all respects. He distributed charity to the sutas, the magadhas, the vandis, and men of all other professions, according to their educational qualifications, and satisfied everyone's desires.

-(Srimad Bhagavatam, Canto-10, Chapter-5)

Cow In Vedas
There Is No Wealth Whatsoever Like Cows

तृणानि   खादन्ति   वसन्त्यरण्ये   पिबन्ति   तोयान्यपरिग्रहाणि।
दुहन्ति   वाहन्ति   पुनन्ति   पापं   गवां   रसैर्जीवति   जीवलोक: ॥
तुष्टास्तु   गाव: शमयन्ति   पापं   दत्तास्तु   गावस्त्रिदिवं   नयन्ति।
संरक्षिताश्चोपनयन्ति   वित्तं   गोभिर्न   तुल्यं   धनमस्ति   किंचित्॥
शष्यं   समश्नाति   ददाति   नित्यं   पापापहं   मित्रविवर्धनं   च।
स   एव   चाऽऽर्य: परिभुज्यते   च   गोभिर्न   तुल्यं   धनमस्ति   किंचित्॥
तृणानि   शुष्कानि   वने   चरित्वा   पीत्वापि   तोयान्यमृतं   स्रवन्ति।
यद्रोमयाद्याश्च   पुनन्ति   लोकान्   गोभिर्न   तुल्यं   धनमस्ति   किंचित्॥

Cows live in forest, eat grass, drink water here and there, give us milk, carry our goods, dispel our sins and sustain the life of living beings by gorasa, the milk.

When pleased by service, they destroy our sinful reactions. When given in charity, they lead us to heavenly planets. When cared for properly, cows are wealth personified. There is no wealth whatsoever like cows.

In exchange of ordinary grass, cow gives countless bounties. Cow is an engine of peace and prosperity in society. Bull sustains the creation by ploughing the fields. The worlds subsist on grain grown by the bull. There is no wealth whatsoever like cows.

Feeding on dry straw and drinking water from ditches, cows deliver the elixir of life, milk. Cows purify the three worlds with gomaya and gomutra (cow dung and urine). There is no wealth whatsoever like cows.

3.

Cow

A Life Form For All-round Good Of The World

Cattle occupy a unique role in human history and many cultures consider cattle the oldest form of wealth, and cattle raiding consequently is one of the earliest forms of theft.

Many of the problems we are now facing, including violence and wars, are a direct result of the massive animal killing going on everywhere. We don't connect it. It's karma. When we do something violent to another living entity, the violence comes back to us. It's like bouncing a ball off the ground. Scientists can relate to the natural forces at work in the bouncing ball but they can not see the forces acting on a more subtle level.

People Just Don't Think About It!

People just don't think about it. Even when we are young, our mother always lovingly served us meat and potatoes and encouraged us to dine heartily on the carcass so we could "grow up big and strong." And the TV adds and the billboards daily reinforce the conditioning that it's "perfectly normal" to kill animals for food. So most never question it; they don't make the connection between the seemingly innocent hamburger on their plate and the horror of the slaughterhouse. Out of sight, out of mind.

But the fact is, to satisfy our corrupted appetites, billions of animals are unnecessarily and brutally butchered every year. And year after year this inhumanity continues to be overlooked.

Is it right that animals, fully sentient beings, are made to suffer simply because we "like the taste?" Has selfishness overcome our reason? We've got blood on our hands. It's no wonder there is so much violence in our society when we exhibit so much violence towards animals. "What goes around comes around."

Cow And World's Well-being

Cow is a life form meant for all round good of the world. It's something like a mother whose every gesture is for the good of the child. Cow protection ensures world's well-being in all respects - economic, social, environmental, ecological, physical, political, intellectual, moral, cultural and emotional.

Modern civilization has made considerable advances in the fields of science and technology but the world has not become a better place to live. Rather the opposite is true.

If we study the life of a typical villager in any traditional community, we may find him living with his wife and a few children in a thatched hut with mud walls and a dirt floor. He has a couple of cows, a well and some land. He may have never gone beyond two or three neighboring villages, but he's happy. He lives to a ripe old age, doesn't get many diseases, works honestly in the fields, and has enough milk and grains to eat. With his extra produce, beyond what he needs to maintain his family, he may trade for clothing, jewelry and other items. In other words, he lives a very simple life. And he has sufficient time in hand to cultivate art, culture and to nurture the tradition, in a crime and stress free environment. Now this 'backward and undeveloped' community needs to be developed and science and technology need to be introduced in their lives. Soon they will be a 'developed' lot with pollution, crime, stress, life-style diseases, family breakdown, drugs, violence, prostitution and financial meltdowns. This is what is being done to our world in the name of progress and development.

A world that has moved away from cow protection and resorted to

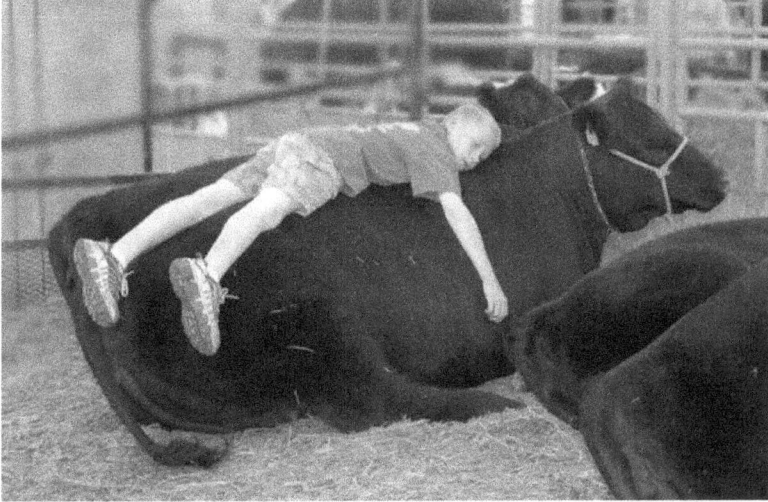

indiscriminate cow killing is not happier. In fact it is a lot less happier than its ancestors who were seemingly bereft of plasma TVs, touch screen ipods and 6mm laptops. Of course, these ancestors (who were not in Vedic tradition) might have killed cows but cows were never a staple.

Its interesting to note that pastoral communities have highly developed art, culture and music. Cowherds are good at playing flutes and other instruments. In a stress free life, living with gentle animals, they can afford to play flute while doing their "job". Imagine doing it while sitting on a computer terminal for ten hours a day or while steering a monstrous truck, darting on an expressway. Modern industrialized living kills all finer instincts and promotes bestial passions.

World Progress Under Scanner

World progress has increasingly come under scanner of late. The question being asked has three dimensions - first whether we have

"...the gentle, large-brained, social cow, that caresses our hands and face with her rough tongue, and is more like man's sister than any other non-human being—the majestic, beautiful creature with the Juno eyes..."
- W. H. Hudson,

really made progress when progress is taken to mean overall well being and happiness of society. Secondly whether the progress has been in the right direction? While busy looking at the speedometer, have we missed the milestone? What would be the use of speeding along if the road we have taken is the wrong one. Thirdly, whether the so called progress is really required?

It is a fact that as we have progressed, our interaction with animal kingdom and nature in general has reduced. Most people's association with cow is on the dinner table and association with nature is a 'nature' wallpaper on their desktop. A society thus disconnected is a disoriented society.

A cow or bull may appear like dumb beasts, but inside that hide and muscle is a sentient soul who knows pleasure and pain, contentment and anger. God has placed these loving animals here not to become our food, but to provide us with milk and to labor for us just as a father or mother would work for the family. Like a mother, the cow supplies milk, and like a father the ox tills the ground.

Progress of A Slaughterhouse Society - Towards Hell

A society, which resorts to indiscriminate killing, especially of cows and bulls can never be happy. Nature strikes back for all the slaughter, the Vedic scriptures say, with incurable disease and war and host of other problems. A society can never be happy by killing its mother and father.

In 2002, Australian liberal political theorist Clive Hamilton published a book by the name Growth Fetish which became a best-seller in Australia. The book has been the subject of much controversy, and has managed to infuriate commentators on both the left and right of the politico-economic debate.

The thesis of the book is that the policies of unfettered capitalism pursued by the west for the last 50 years have largely failed, since the underlying purpose of the creation of wealth is happiness, and Hamilton contends that people in general are no happier now than 50 years ago, despite the huge increase in personal wealth. In fact, he suggests that the reverse is true. Hamilton also proposes that the pursuit of growth has been at a tremendous cost in terms of the environment, erosion of democracy, and the values of society as a whole, as well as not delivering the hoped for increases in personal happiness. One result is that we, as a society, have become obsessed with materialism and consumerism. Hamilton's catchphrase "People buy things they don't want, with money they don't have, to impress people they don't like" neatly sums up his philosophy on progress.

When a doctor sees a patient's vital signs going off the chart, he knows it's time for emergency medication, perhaps too late. But what about a society? A chart of mankind's vital signs over the last thousand years would look like a patient going terminal. Take whatever indicator you like - environment, ethics, crime, energy consumption, CO_2 emissions - and graph it. The left three-fourths of the chart would be almost a horizontal line, followed by an almost vertical line covering the last 200 years. Is it time for remedial action?

We have come to think of growth as the Great Benefactor. Rapid growth has been the hallmark of the industrialized world, bestowing on its lucky denizens a standard of living unmatched in human history. Governments of every creed - capitalist, communist, Islamic, whatever - strive to promote ever greater economic growth. But should we be thinking of growth not as the Great Benefactor but as the Great Destroyer? Has growth become like a malignant cancer, devouring the very body which sustains it? Yes! Because this so called growth is at the cost of poor animals' lives. Killing more animals, eating more flesh, is an accompanying characteristic of any nation's growth. Affluence immediately reflects in changes in dietary patterns.

Modernization means more cruelty, more apathy and less consideration for animal rights. Mechanized slaughter and factory farming is a result of our scientific, technological and economic progress, simply resulting in more suffering for the animals. Inflicting pain and sorrows is hardly a way to achieve peace and happiness.

Our so called growth or progress is simply our march towards hell. History is a witness to this fact and history always repeats itself.

Cheerful Cows - A Sign of A Happy Society

In the latest Happy Planet Index (HPI) survey, the U.K. settled at 41st, ahead of all other G8 nations and the U.S. came in 105th. Some of the poorest countries like Vietnam topped the list. Here we see that happiness is not a function of economic growth.

In fact, because of the dramatic increase in rape, incest, murder, violent crime, theft, stress and child abuse, people are generally in a state of great anxiety.

Industrialized societies are the worst affected. Social systems are crumbling and people are living under great duress. 33% of the US population needs psychiatric intervention at some point or another. One in three is going nuts and they say, "If two of your friends are normal, you better watch out!"

Could it be the karma for all the killing and crimes against creation. It appears so. In Vedic conception, condition of cows and bulls reflects the condition of the society.

Srimad Bhagavatam describes the rule of Pandava dynasty:

"During the reign of Maharaja Yudhisthira, the clouds showered all the water that people needed, and the earth produced all the necessities of man in profusion. Due to its fatty milk bag and cheerful attitude, the cow used to moisten the grazing ground with milk."(SB 1.10.4)

Srila Prabhupada comments on this verse:

"The basic principle of economic development is centered on land and cows. The necessities of human society are food grains, fruits, milk, minerals, clothing, wood, etc. One requires all these items to fulfill the material needs of the body. Certainly one does not require flesh and fish or iron tools and machinery. During the regime of Maharaja Yudhisthira, all over the world there were regulated rainfalls. Rainfalls are not in the control of the human being. The heavenly King Indradeva is the controller of rains, and he is the servant of the Lord. When the Lord is obeyed by the king and the people under the King's administration, there are regulated rains from the horizon, and these rains are the causes of all varieties of production on the land. Not only do regulated rains help ample production of grains and fruits, but when they combine with astronomical influences there is ample production of valuable stones and pearls. Grains and vegetables can sumptuously feed a man and animals, and a fatty cow delivers enough milk to supply a man sumptuously with vigor and vitality. If there is enough milk, enough grains, enough fruit, enough cotton, enough silk and enough jewels, then why do the people need cinemas, houses of prostitution, slaughterhouses, etc.? What is the need of an artificial luxurious life of cinema, cars, radio, flesh and hotels? Has this civilization produced anything but quarreling individually and nationally? Has this civilization enhanced the cause of equality and fraternity by sending thousands of men into a hellish factory and the war fields at the whims of a particular man?"

Solve your problem like... Produce your food wherever you are there. Till little, little labor, and you will get your whole year's food. And distribute the food to the animal, cow, and eat yourself. The cow will eat the refuse. You take the rice, and the skin you give to the cow. From dahl you take the grain, and the skin you give to the... And fruit, you take the fruit, and the skin you give to the cow, and he will give you milk. So why should you kill him? Milk is the miraculous food; therefore Ksrna says krsi-go-raksya vanijyam [Bg. 18.44]. Give protection to the cow, take milk from it, and eat food grains—your food problem is solved. Where is food problem? Why should you invent such civilization always full of anxieties, running the car here and there, and fight with other nation..? What is this civilization?
-Srila Prabhupada

"It is said here that the cows used to moisten the pasturing land with milk because their milk bags were fatty and the animals were joyful. Do they not require, therefore, proper protection for a joyful life by being fed with a sufficient quantity of grass in the field? Why should men kill cows for their selfish purposes? Why should man not be satisfied with grains, fruits and milk, which, combined together, can produce hundreds and thousands of palatable dishes. Why are there slaughterhouses all over the world to kill innocent animals? Maharaja Pariksit, grandson of Maharaja Yudhisthira, while touring his vast kingdom, saw a black man attempting to kill a cow. The King at once arrested the butcher and chastised him sufficiently. Should not a king or executive head protect the lives of the poor animals who are unable to defend themselves? Is this humanity? Are not the animals of a country citizens also? Then why are they allowed to be butchered in organized slaughterhouses? Are these the signs of equality, fraternity and nonviolence?"

The Vedic civilization, the brahmanas, they used to live in the forest, and the king would offer them some cows. So they will draw some milk. And in the forest there are fruits, so they will eat fruits and milk. And if the disciples go to the village, beg some food grain, then sometimes they cook some food grains. Otherwise the brahmanas used to live in the forest, drink milk and take fruit. That is sufficient. There was no need of jumping here and there. Anywhere you keep cows. And what cows to maintain? No expenditure. The fruits? The skin thrown away, and the cow will eat. And in exchange it will give you nice foodstuff, milk. Or it will eat in the grazing ground, some grass. So there is no expenditure of keeping cows, but you get the best food in the world. The proof is that the child born simply can live on milk. That is the proof. So anyone can live only on milk. If you have got the opportunity to drink one pound milk maximum, not very much -- half-pound is sufficient; suppose one pound -- then you don't require any other foodstuff. Only this cow's milk will help you. It is so nice. And it gives very nice brain, not pig's brain. So it is so important thing.
-Srila Prabhupada (Srimad-Bhagavatam 6.1.21 -- Honolulu, May 21, 1976)

"Therefore, in contrast with the modern, advanced, civilized form of government, an autocracy like Maharaja Yudhisthira's is by far superior to a so-called democracy in which animals are killed and a man less than an animal is allowed to cast votes for another less-than-animal man."

"We are all creatures of material nature. In the Bhagavad-gita it is said that the Lord Himself is the seed-giving father and material nature is the mother of all living beings in all shapes. Thus mother material nature has enough foodstuff both for animals and for men, by the grace of the Father Almighty, Sri Krsna. The human being is the elder brother of all other living beings. He is endowed with intelligence more powerful than animals for realizing the course of nature and the indications of the Almighty Father. Human civilizations should depend on the production of material nature without artificially attempting economic development to turn the world into a chaos of artificial greed and power only for the purpose of artificial luxuries and sense gratification. This is but the life of dogs and hogs." (Purport, SB 1.10.4) (© BBTI)

Ox - A Founding Father of Modern Nations
A Symbol of Our Slower, Saner Past

Sturdy, earthy, no-nonsense - that's an Ox. Affectionate and easy-going, the ox can show a fierce temper when agitated. He is neat, tidy and quiet animal and enjoys plodding along from day to day without griping or complaining. A symbol of quiet strength and unassuming kindness, ox is noted for his ability to work hard without breaking a sweat, a life form dedicated for well-being of others.

The ox is the sign of prosperity through fortitude and hard work. To say that the humble "ox" played a pivotal role in world history might to some appear rather strange, but to the people of Salzberg, this beast is a symbol of courage in the face of adversity.

In the 1500s, an enemy army laid a seize to the city of Salzburg in Austria, depriving the inhabitants of food and drink. Their cupboards bare with nary a bit of food left, the people were practically ready to surrender until they found a lone ox roaming the streets. They paraded the beast in front of the invaders to prove that they were not hungry. Then, during the night, they painted it black to show that they had more than enough food for the people to survive as testified by the living bull. Completely confused, the army retreated, leaving the people of Salzberg in peace.

Beneath the placid, easy-going and unpretentious exterior of the ox lies a kind heart, a modest amount of ambition, and a willingness to bear heavy burdens that might overwhelm others, not to mention a strong sense of loyalty. This is a revered animal who symbolizes diligence, reliability, sincerity, strength and sound judgment. But don't expect these lumbering souls to have a sparkling sense of humor or be at all style conscious.

For centuries and millenniums, ox has been used for plowing, logging, parades, religious ceremonies, sports (in pulling or driving contests), general farm work or simply as a pack animal (an animal that carries cargo on its back).

Male oxen are typically castrated (sexually neutered by the removal

64

of testes) to produce a larger, stronger, and more docile animal. If we take the archeological evidence, for over 6000 years, the world has utilized this gentle soul to represent the muscle of civilization. How much obliged the humanity should be towards this creature for all the services rendered all along.

Great nations of the world owe a lot to the ox. Oxen hauled carts loaded with crops from the fields to barns and to markets, pulled plows in fields, and turned wheels that lifted water from wells and canals. The ox also was used to pack personal property. So essential was the ox for the survival that it was worshiped in many cultures. For thousands of years, the ox remained the primary draft animal on farms in most parts of the world.

Ox is one of the founding fathers of the great land of America. Oxen pulled the covered wagons west. Oxen helped clear the land. In the 19th century the ox was the preferred draft animal for pulling covered wagons over pioneer trails across the western United States. Ox was stronger and less expensive to maintain than a horse, and could live off the grass and foliage along the way. Unlike a horse or a mule, an ox pulled wagons through mud and swam across streams. The ox was slower than a mule, but it pulled at a steady pace and would travel a greater distance than a mule during a full day of travel.

Today oxen are our link to a slower and probably a saner past.

Ox vs. Tractor

The first engine-powered farm tractors used steam and were introduced in 1868. These engines were built as small road locomotives and were used for general road haulage and in particular by the timber trade. Charter Gasoline Engine Company of Illinois was the first company to successfully use gasoline as fuel. Charter's creation of a gasoline fueled engine in 1887 soon led to early gasoline traction engines before the term "tractor" was coined by others.

John Froelich, a thresherman from Iowa, tried gasoline power for threshing for the first time in 1892. He mounted a Van Duzen gasoline engine on a Robinson chassis and rigged his own gearing for propulsion. Froelich used the machine successfully to power a threshing machine by belt during his fifty-two day harvest season in South Dakota. The Froelich tractor is considered by many to be the first successful gasoline tractor known.

One Mr. Hart-Parr is credited with coining the word "tractor" for machines that had previously been called gas traction engines. The firm's first tractor effort, Hart-Parr No.1, was made in 1901.

However, it wasn't until 1910 that gasoline powered tractors came to be used extensively in farming. It was Henry Ford who produced his first experimental gasoline powered tractor in 1907. It was referred to as an "automobile plow" and the name tractor was not used.

Farm mechanization is just over a hundred year old story. Before that all the work was done by the draught animals. As long as cheap oil is available, we can safely eat these poor animals but what after that?

Replacement of Ox With Machinery

An Indian Case Study

Farming methods based on draught animals are among the most significant agricultural systems in the world. In the production of rice and other crops in the tropics these systems remain critical to the food security of expanding populations. They are a major contributor to employment and a major source of income from crop products, calves, animal rental and animal by-products.

After independence, Indian government made efforts in earnest to promote farm mechanisation through tractors. But the question remains, can tractors completely replace draught animals?

Small and marginal farmers comprise over 80 per cent of cultivators in India. They can not afford tractors. Average farm size, too, is becoming smaller due to fragmentation. Besides, difficult terrain in several regions (say, hilly areas) prevents tractor use. So, exactly how viable is the small tractor for such farmers?

A single fact could clinch this argument. Draught animal population in India has been steadily declining (see table below). Government has poorly invested in research on draught animals. The only time a concerted effort occurred was in the mid-1980s, propelled by sizeable funding from foreign and multilateral sources, alarmed at the African food crisis (the absence of draught animals in sub-Saharan Africa meant that ploughs were pulled by humans).

India has always had the best draught animals. The research funds came to institutions affiliated to the Indian Council for Agricultural Research. By the late 1980s, research papers were generated highlighting the most critical issues in the draught animals sector. This was also the time when the value of draft animals to Indian economy was calculated and understood. In 1987, a national seminar was held on draught animal power at the Central Institute of Agricultural Engineering (CIAE), Bhopal.

As soon as there is discrepancy in the protection of cows, there will be no more peace in the world. - Srila Prabhupada (Lecture , Los Angeles, December 4, 1968)

Reducing Population of Draught animals in field operations in India (in million)

Livestock		1971-72	1981-82	1990-91	1991-92	1996-97
Cattle	Male	72.56	61.05	61.62	61.1	58.53
	Female	2.07	2.04	1.92	1.91	1.87

Source: Agricultural Research Data Book, 2001

Death of Draught Breeds - Death of A Renewable Energy Source

India had the world's best draught animals, particularly oxen ('India carriers Inc', Down To Earth, June 15, 2000). They were promoted in pre-Independence India by princely states and temple trusts, which provided funds to develop specialised breeds as well as stud bulls for breed improvement in villages.

Of India's 27 known cattle breeds, most were developed for draught in times the economy ran on animal power. Milk production wasn't the focus of cattle breeding, then. With the Green Revolution, it was assumed tractors would make draught animals irrelevant. Government support for breed maintenance died out. Provisional figures for the 2003 Livestock Census show indigenous cattle have decreased by 13 per cent from 1992. Crossbred cattle have increased by 46 per cent. So much so, most indigenous cattle '80-90 percent' is now categorised as 'non-descript'.

With the White Revolution, milch cattle were its backbone, the breeding emphasis changed. Breeding programmes turned into crossbreeding with exotic cattle. Meant to improve 'non-descript' animals, it led to the genetic decimation of the best draught breeds ('Vanishing breeds', Down To Earth, September 15, 1997).

The most serious challenge today is the loss of the genetic base of draught animals, point out animal breeders. It is very easy to develop milch breeds, for the output is easy to calculate in terms of quality as well as quantity. Developing draught breeds is several times more difficult: the criteria for measuring are not very clear. Breeding experiments with draught animals probably don't exist anywhere in the world.

One way to maintain the draught breeds would have been to tap into foreign markets. After all, didn't the research funding come as a result of the African farm power crisis? But India hasn't exported draught animals to Africa; it hasn't developed any market for draught breeds at all, with or without the support of development agencies. Brazilian breeders can often be sighted in Indian cattle fairs, selecting animals of fast-growing breeds that possess resistance to diseases; does the government know this? Is it prepared to respond to such interest, via a full-blown strategy? In fact, one of India's leading business houses with expertise in cattle breeding has been seeking a license to export embryos of the Ongole, the largest cattle breed in the world, native to Ongole in Andhra Pradesh. But the Union ministry of agriculture's department of animal husbandry and dairying has steadily refused. The department has a breed conservation plan of its own, which is ineffective. On top of that, it prevents efforts to profit from draught breed conservation. The losers, ultimately, are small farmers.

Mahatma Gandhi's program was village organization of which cow protection was an integral part. But leaders like Nehru had their 'made in London' ideas. These copy cats didn't realize that one man's food is another man's poison. London owed its economic success to centuries of plunder and Indian conditions were completely different.

At the moment, India is pursuing made in Italy ideas. Turn all the cows into beef pasta. These shortsighted government planners are unaware of the implications of post peak oil situation. A country like India which depends on agriculture in all respects would run into serious difficulties if petroleum prices skyrocket.

Ox Power Is Humanity's Futures

Animal power should remain an integral part of strategies for rural development and agricultural modernization. Even though agriculture is undergoing modernization in many areas, the use of draught animals persists and even expanding

Throughout the developing world - and in many developed countries as well - draught animals are an inseparable part of agriculture. Oxen and to some extant other animals like buffaloes, horses, mules, donkeys and camels are used in ploughing, planting and weeding, transportation of produce, water and fuelwood, and for water-lifting, logging and land excavation.

Food And Agriculture Organization of The United Nations (FAO)'s Agricultural Engineering Branch (AGSE) reports that in sub-Saharan Africa in particular, the use of work animals for agriculture and rural transport is increasing every year. In countries that are rapidly urbanizing and industrializing - such as India, Mexico, Brazil and South Africa - large-scale farms may use tractors and trucks, but many small-scale farmers and local transporters continue to use animals. "This pattern of mechanized large farms and animal-powered small farms is common worldwide," the AGSE report says. "Even in the highly developed European Union, animal power remains important in Spain, Portugal and Greece, where farms are of small size. In the USA, Amish farmers run their farms profitably using only animal power."

But draught animals have an "image problem". Over the past fifty years, books on farming - whether for school children or agricultural students - have presented gleaming new tractors, rather than sturdy oxen and hardy donkeys, as the solution to on-farm power needs. Result: most teachers, researchers and decision-makers have never studied animal power in detail. Their ignorance is compounded by popular media, which portray animal power as an old - and inherently poor - technology.

AGSE recommends a fresh look at the benefits of draught animals: "Animal power is generally affordable and accessible to the smallholder farmers, who are responsible for much of the world's food production. Studies show that individual tractor ownership is seldom possible for farmers with small areas of cultivation, unless they have high-value crops, irrigation and/or multiple cropping (e.g., irrigated rice production). Tractor hire is seldom viable for smallholders in rain-fed food production systems. While tractors are better adapted for power-intensive operations, such as ploughing, and for large areas of land, animals may be more appropriate and affordable for control-intensive operations (e.g., weeding) and on small areas of land."

The use of draught animals carries economic benefits well beyond the farm gate. Animal power requires little or no foreign exchange - money invested in animal power circulates within rural areas, helping to revitalise rural economies. Pack animals and carts facilitate the marketing of produce, stimulating local trade. Animals can also provide important local "feeder" transport between farms and roads, thus complementing motorized road transport systems.

Finally, animal power is sustainable and environmentally friendly. "It is a renewable energy source that can be sustained with little external input," AGSE notes. "The use of animal power in mixed farming systems encourages crop-livestock integration and sustainable farming practices. Not only do work animals produce their own organic manure, they provide transport to the fields of manure of other livestock, which enhances the fertility and structure of the soil."

Animal Power Networks

Several countries have established formal or informal national animal power networks to exchange experiences, skills and materials through workshops, publications and cooperative programmes. Important international networks include the Animal Traction Network for Eastern and Southern Africa (ATNESA) and the Red Latinoamericana de Tracción Animal (RELATA, relata@ibw.com.ni).

To fully harness the benefits of animal power it should be seen as an integral component of rural development and agricultural mechanization strategies. Animal power options need to be considered in plans relating to food security, rural infrastructure and services and transport. At present, transport ministries seldom deal with animal power, even though pack animals or carts are often the mainstay of rural transport systems. Similarly, using animals for labour-intensive road construction can be highly cost-effective, but engineers are usually trained to plan capital-intensive projects.

Experience of many countries shows that animal power can be developed and sustained by small-scale private sector enterprises. Governments and development agencies should ensure, therefore, a policy environment that enables private sector support services to continue and expand. "Legislation or development processes should not isolate animal power users or support services, either directly or indirectly," AGSE cautions. "Recent examples of marginalization include subsidies on alternative power sources (notably tractors and imported equipment), exclusion of animal-powered transport, and laws more favourable to factories than village blacksmiths."

Above all, animal power needs to develop and evolve. The technology should not remain static, but respond to innovations and new challenges. Since animal traction has been largely neglected, there is need for basic scientific research relating to work animals, harnessing and implements.

Finally, AGSE says, "it's time to polish the popular image of those hard-working Oxen, buffaloes, horses, mules, donkeys and camels: Increasingly, the constraints to animal power development are psychological or social rather than technical or economic. There is need to counteract existing negative and outmoded media coverage if people are to consider animal power as a realistic option. Animal traction needs to be portrayed as a renewable, environmentally friendly technology that enhances the quality of community life and is relevant to the modern world."

Cuba - Taking The Lead

In Cuba, the ox is mightier than the tractor. Ox is viewed as way to ramp up food production while conserving energy. Cuba relies more heavily than ever on oxen to save fuel normally used by heavily machinery.

President Castro recently suggested expanding a pilot program that gives private farmers fallow government land to cultivate — but without the use of gas-guzzling machinery.

"For this program we should forget about tractors and fuel, even if we had enough. The idea is to work basically with oxen," Castro told parliament on Aug. 1, 2009. "An increasing number of growers have been doing exactly this with excellent results."

Though the island gets nearly 100,000 free barrels of oil a day from Venezuela, it also has begun a campaign to conserve crude. The agricultural ministry in late June proposed increasing the use of oxen to save fuel. The ministry said it had more than 265,000 oxen "capable of matching, and in some cases overtaking, machines in labor load and planting."

In the farming initiative that began last year, about 82,000 applicants have received more than 1.7 million acres so far — or 40 percent of the government's formerly idle land. Shortages in Cuba are not new. And neither are oxen. Thousands of Cuban farmers have relied on the beasts in the half century since Fidel and Raul Castro took over the country. "The ox means so much to us. Without oxen farming is not farming," says Omar Andalio, 37, as he carefully coaxes a pair of government-owned beasts through a sugarcane field.

Plain Living High Thinking Farming Communities
An Alternative To The Modern Slaughterhouse Civilization

Plain living high thinking farming communities provide the time-honored alternative to the modern slaughterhouse civilization.

It is possible to live a comfortable, simple life in harmony with nature. All that is required is some land, cows and food grains. With these three necessities we can obtain everything required for a simple life. A simple life like that doesn't mean uncomfortable life, and that it is a practical alternative to todays hectic city life.

It's strange that in our high-tech society, despite modern time-saving devices, it seems most people have little time to do anything except eat, sleep and work.

Many people spend the majority of their waking hours traveling to and fro and working in a job simply to pay the bills. If there is some spare time then "getting out of it" at the bar, watching television or taking one of the many recreational drugs seem to be high priority activities.

On a plain living and high thinking farm community, there are no bills to pay. Everything can be produced from the land. Excess produce can be sold or traded for small requirements of money.

The plain living and high thinking communities provide an alternative lifestyle with ample time for enquiring into the meaning of life. Also this is an ideal place for artists, craftspersons, writers and musicians to work.

Plain Living and High Thinking — A Solution to the Unemployment Problem

Technology has manufactured tractors and computers, however it has failed to manufacture jobs for the people displaced by these wonders. There are certainly many new opportunities in the high-tech world for intelligent technologists, however not everyone is so intelligent.

Each person has different levels and types of skills and abilities. A just society should provide suitable work for everyone according to their ability. Technology has abolished much of the traditional work. This means the displaced workers must swell the ranks of the unemployed, or take employment in areas not really suited to their ability. For many of the young unemployed there is little future, so they are resorting to alcohol and drugs to "dull the pain."

We are losing a whole generation of young people simply because

In the beginning there is plot of land and a cow— your whole economic question is solved. Why you should work so hard day and night? So we have created a civilization simply working hard day and night, and the purpose is sense gratification. That's all. That is prohibited. Make your life simplified. Save your time for Krsna consciousness. That is the program. Don't be implicated with sinful activities. Simple life.
-Srila Prabhupada (Srimad-Bhagavatam 5:5:1, Los Angeles, January 20, 1969)

we are unable to employ them in any useful way. A large percentage of young people are now unemployed. Even amongst the employed many are being exploited in "dead end" jobs such as cash register operators in supermarkets, only to be thrown away when they become too old.

In this throw away society it seems that we are now happy to throw away an entire generation of the young.

The plain living and high thinking communities can provide a practical solution for this rejected generation by giving them an opportunity to engage in meaningful work, according to their ability. This will enable them to regain their dignity and sense of purpose in life.

God Made the Country, Man Made the City

The country and the forests are in the mode of goodness and therefore provide the perfect atmosphere for those interested in developing the spiritual aspects of life. There is a type of peace available in the country that no city dweller could dream of. City life is in the mode of passion and ignorance and the city dwellers is automatically affected by these modes.

There is urgent need to establish more and more God centred plain living and high thinking communities to give people a chance to take a break from their high-pressure, smog filled environments for at least some time. Even if they only spend a week or a weekend living in the community, they will be benefited.

If there are cows, land and a store of food grains we have everything needed for a comfortable life. Regardless of what is going on in the rest of the world the cows can be milked, the land can be cultivated with the assistance of the bulls and delicious foodstuffs can be prepared from the milk products and grains.

The businessman with a big bank balance and a factory producing nuts and bolts can't eat the nuts and bolts and at any moment his fortune in the bank can become worthless. In contrast the Plain Living and High Thinking farmer with cows, grains and land has real, practical wealth which will not be lost in times of economic crisis.

(From Changing the Face of the Earth Campaign)

Cow & World Peace

We can remain in peace as long as we let others live in peace. If we are not willing to spare peace, we need not expect peace. Those who clamor for peace should know that animals have as much right to exist in God's creation as we have. Human wrongs can never undermine animal rights.

Srila Prabhupada explains, "The bull is the emblem of the moral principle, and the cow is the representative of the earth. When the bull and the cow are in a joyful mood, it is to be understood that the people of the world are also in a joyful mood. The reason is that the bull helps production of grains in the agricultural field, and the cow delivers milk, the miracle of aggregate food values. The human society, therefore, maintains these two important animals very carefully so that they can wander everywhere in cheerfulness. But at the present moment in this age of Kali both the bull and the cow are now being slaughtered and eaten up as foodstuff by a class of men who do not know the brahminical culture. The bull and the cow can be protected for the good of all human society simply by the spreading of brahminical culture as the topmost perfection of all cultural affairs. By advancement of such culture, the morale of society is properly maintained, and so peace and prosperity are also attained without extraneous effort." (Srimad Bhagavatam 1.16.18)

Srila Prabhupada adds, "The next symptom of the age of Kali is the distressed condition of the cow. Milking the cow means drawing the

"Why injustice? These poor animals, they are also my subject. How you can kill them? He's also born in this land." "National" means one is born in that particular land. So they are also born in this land. Why he should be treated differently? Just like in your country, even one Indian gets his child here, the child is counted as USA-born, US citizen, Immediately. So if that is the law, that anyone born in this land should be treated as national, what is this law that the cows and the bulls born in that land, they are to be slaughtered? What is this law?"

-Srila Prabhupada (Srimad-Bhagavatam 1.16.4, Los Angeles, January 1, 1974)

principles of religion in a liquid form. The great risis and munis would live only on milk. Srila Sukadeva Gosvami would go to a householder while he was milking a cow, and he would simply take a little quantity of it for subsistence. Even fifty years ago, no one would deprive a sadhu of a quart or two of milk, and every householder would give milk like water. For a Sanatanist (a follower of Vedic principles) it is the duty of every householder to have cows and bulls as household paraphernalia, not only for drinking milk, but also for deriving religious principles. The Sanatanist worships cows on religious principles and respects brahmanas. The cow's milk is required for the sacrificial fire, and by performing sacrifices the householder can be happy. The cow's calf not only is beautiful to look at, but also gives satisfaction to the cow, and so she delivers as much milk as possible. But in the Kali-yuga, the calves are separated from the cows as early as possible for purposes which may not be mentioned in these pages of Srimad-Bhagavatam. The cow stands with tears in her eyes, the sudra milkman draws milk from the cow artificially, and when there is no milk the cow is sent to be slaughtered. These greatly sinful acts are responsible for all the troubles in present society. People do not know what they are doing in the name of economic development. The influence of Kali will keep them in the darkness of ignorance. Despite all endeavors for peace and prosperity, they must try to see the cows and the bulls happy in all respects. Foolish people do not

know how one earns happiness by making the cows and bulls happy, but it is a fact by the law of nature. Let us take it from the authority of Srimad-Bhagavatam and adopt the principles for the total happiness of humanity. (SB 1.17.3)

Srila Prabhupada further continues, "Panca-gavya, the five products received from the cow, namely milk, yogurt, ghee, cow dung and cow urine, are required in all ritualistic ceremonies performed according to the Vedic directions. Cow urine and cow dung are uncontaminated, and since even the urine and dung of a cow are important, we can just imagine how important this animal is for human civilization. Therefore the Supreme Personality of Godhead, Krsna, directly advocates go-raksya, the protection of cows. Civilized men who follow the system of varnasrama, especially those of the vaisya class, who engage in agriculture and trade, must give protection to the cows. Unfortunately, because people in Kali-yuga are mandah, all bad, and sumanda-matayah, misled by false conceptions of life, they are killing cows in the thousands. Therefore they are deficient in spiritual consciousness, and nature disturbs them in so many ways, especially through incurable diseases like cancer and through frequent wars among nations. As long as human society continues to allow cows to be regularly killed in slaughterhouses, there cannot be any question of peace and prosperity." (SB 8.8.11)

The friendly cow, all red and white,
I love with all my heart:
She gives me cream with all her might,
To eat with apple-tart.

~Robert Louis Stevenson (1850-1894)

4.
Cow Provides Ground
For Cultivation Of Human Spirit

One of the significant developments of the last 50 years has been the dramatic shift away from ethical-religious values that provide the foundation for any civilization. A whole generation of younger section seems oblivious to the concern. While some analysts realize why this is occurring, most have no idea where these changes will lead to.

For vast majority of the people, the qualities of honesty, sincerity and having high moral standards are no longer valued. For them these are meaningless qualities which have no relevance in the present day world. People are increasingly mired in selfishness, corruption, knavery

The cow to me means the entire sub-human world, extending man's sympathies beyond his own species. Man through the cow is enjoined to realize his identity with all that lives. Why the ancient rishis selected the cow for apotheosis is obvious to me. The cow in India was the best comparison; she was the giver of plenty. Not only did she give milk, but she also made agriculture possible. The cow is a poem of pity; one reads pity in the gentle animal. She is the second mother to millions of mankind. Protection of the cow means protection of the whole dumb creation of God. The appeal of the lower order of creation is all the more forceful because it is speechless. -Gandhi

and other wrong doings. Today one can do anything to meet his or her narrow ends. The pace at which people are giving up their values, future of human society remains a debatable topic.

There is an explosion of immorality and moral standards are falling fast and inexorably to barbarity. Media which controls the popular mind set has become increasingly callous and hostile to ethical-religious values. Public schools today demand value-neutrality. Religious leaders are increasingly prone to ambiguity and compromise in vital areas of doctrine and morals. State has outlawed God in public places while claiming 'In God We Trust'.

The result has been a surge in divorce, cohabitation, sexual promiscuity, perversion, teen pregnancy, abortions, child abuse, drug abuse, rape, cheating, shoplifting, embezzling, bankruptcy, incivility, and violent crimes - the very things God prophesied would happen to nations that forsake His laws.

Public today is condoning or at least is nonjudgemental about behavior long considered disgraceful and immoral.

What about personal character? Take the example of a former US President who had his lawyers seeking an out-of-court settlement on charges of indecent exposure, not to mention presiding over a scandal-a-day administration. Yet he received high approval ratings from the general population. The fact that he became president, was re-elected and retains a high approval rating does say something about the new standards people have for what's acceptable conduct. This is probably the first time in history that a open womanizer could have been elected and re-elected president, and, in the face of one scandal after another, get high public-approval ratings.

> *"Cows are my passion. What I have ever sighed for has been to retreat to a Swiss farm, and live entirely surrounded by cows."*
> *-Charles Dickens*

Then there is French President Nicolas Sarkozy, who is living with a former model. When he was scheduled to visit some Asian countries with his girl friend, the hosting leaders were in a fix. In those parts, cohabiting is considered prostitution. Sensing trouble, President dumped his partner from the tour.

A nude photograph of Carla, France's first lady, has been auctioned for $91,000. To top it all, in what is being called in diplomatic circles an unprecedented move, France's first lady has stripped for a pay-per-view special. Proceeds would go to Somalian kidnappers to secure freedom of hostages aboard a French-owned cruise ship.

Bedlam erupted in the security council chamber of the United Nations as furious diplomats took the government of France to task when the 'Breasts for Hostages' campaign was finally uncovered. Leaders of countries in the southern hemisphere were seen as having no qualms about using their wives in such a manner.

Where are we heading? Most of human behavior cannot and should not be regulated by law. Informal codes of conduct and moral standards provide the glue that holds society together. When these codes and standards, sometimes called traditional values are ignored, trivialized or forgotten, we take another step toward barbarism and incivility.

Does it have to do anything with indiscriminate animal slaughter going all around us? Do our dealings with animals have any bearing on dealings with each other? Do our views on animals and nature in general affect our moral paradigms and social intercourse. How about food? Does it matter in any way in our lives? We will examine these questions next.

tatas canu-dinam dharmah
satyam saucam ksama daya
kalena balina rajan
nanksyaty ayur balam smrtih
Sukadeva Gosvami said: Then, O King, religion, truthfulness,
cleanliness, tolerance, mercy, duration of life, physical strength and
memory will all diminish day by day because of the powerful influence
of the age of Kali.(Srimad Bhagavatam 12.2.1)

Mistreatment of Animals Paves The Way For Crime Against Humanity

There appears to be a direct link between the way people treat animals and the way they treat their fellow human beings.

US serial killer Dennis Rader admitted to police that before he ever started strangling humans, he killed dogs and cats.

As a kid, George Bush enjoyed placing firecrackers on frogs, throwing them in the air, and then watch them blow up. Should this be a cause for alarm? How relevant is a man's childhood behavior to what he is like as an adult? Can we link this childhood behaviour with the heavy bloodshed and wars on terrorism during his tenure.

Cruelty to animals is a common precursor to later criminal violence. George's childhood friend Terry Throckmorton laughingly admits, "We were terrible to animals." So how much importance should we attribute to this early behavior?

Is boy George's lack of empathy and cruelty not just childhood insensitivity, but rather a personality trait still present in the man? If so, we have much to be concerned about. Do we really want a man who appears to be empathetically challenged to hold the most powerful position in America?

Dr. Vizard says, "Cruelty to animals, if accompanied by a sexual interest in animals, is a high-risk indicator of a future sex offender." Studies have shown that individuals who enjoy or are willing to inflict harm on animals are more likely to do so to humans. One of the known warning signs of certain psychopathologies, including antisocial personality disorder, is a history of torturing pets and small animals.

According to the New York Times: "the FBI has found that a history of cruelty to animals is one of the traits that regularly appears in its computer records of serial rapists and murderers, and the standard diagnostic and treatment manual for psychiatric and emotional

I have a terrible image in my mind of a cow going to slaughter. There's not a lot of fight in them. Pigs, they'd squeal and thrash around. They'd fight. It's almost as if cows don't know they have a choice. Not that they don't panic, but they do so in a quiet way." - Cloris Leachman

disorders lists cruelty to animals as a diagnostic criterion for conduct disorders."

Alan R. Felthous reported in his paper "Aggression Against Cats, Dogs, and People" (1980) that: "A survey of psychiatric patients who had repeatedly tortured dogs and cats found all of them had high levels of aggression toward people as well, including one patient who had murdered a boy."

You Are What You Eat

In the Vedic system, foods are categorized according to their bearing on our consciousness. Food is the single most important determinant in how we think, feel and behave.

What to speak of food, even the consciousness of the cook is taken into account; even how the money to buy such food has been earned. Strict vedic adherents will not eat even vegetarian food in the house of some one who is not very clean or whose profession is not very honest.

Slaughterhouse products can destroy all sensitivities and finer sentiments in a human being. A cruel diet of that sort can turn some one into a wild beast. Even wild beasts do not kill unless driven by hunger but human beasts torture and kill simply for recreation. No beast ever mistreats, starves, mutilates, abuses, drugs, cruelly transports and confines another animal.

What you are eating is not a chicken sandwich but a "cruelly-tortured-for-the–entire-life-kept-alive-with–drugs-slaughtered-inhumanely-processed-unsanitarily-and-cooked-at-very-high-temperatures-to-kill-the-salmonella-sandwich.

The famous French philosopher Jean Jacques Rousseau was an advocate of natural order. He observed that the meat eating animals are generally more cruel and violent than herbivores. He therefore reasoned that a vegetarian diet would produce a more compassionate person. He advised that butchers not be allowed to testify in court or sit on juries.

At present, the world is faced with a crisis of unremitting violence in the shape of wars, terrorism, murder, vandalism, child abuse, and abortion. More than 140 wars have been fought since the United Nations was formed in 1945 and in America alone, 55000 people die of gunshots each year. With social and political solutions conspicuously failing, perhaps it's time to analyze the problem from a different perspective - the law of karma. The brutal slaughter of billion of hapless animals must be considered as a powerful causative factor in this.

Animal Killing And Crime Rate

Since 1960, per capita crime rates have more than tripled and so has the meat consumption. May be there is a connection.

Of course the definition of what constitutes a crime depends on the social and political factors in a society, and the nature of crime can change over time. Thirty five years ago, abortion was a crime in almost all the countries including US but now it is perfectly legal to kill babies.

Since 1960, per capita crime rates have more than tripled, while violent crime rates have nearly quintupled. US Department of Justice estimated that 83 percent of all Americans are victims of violent crime at least once in their lives. About a quarter would be victims of three or more violent crimes.

Increasing crime rate means more murders, rapes, robberies,

aggravated assaults, burglaries, and auto thefts. At about 50 per 100,000, Washington DC has the highest murder rate in the developed world.

Violence is also increasing among teenagers and youths. Crime is not a function of poverty but the overall moral fabric of the society. The total number of prisoners in the United States increased from 319,000 in 1980 to 1.3 million in 1999. Another 523,000 people were also in jail. This translates into 1 in every 150 Americans being in prison. The present ratio of the population in prison is more than four times what it was in the mid 1970s. Does it have anything to do with diet? It does. This graph roughly follows the increase in meat consumption during the period.

Superfoods For Super Brains

Cow milk nourishes human brain. Body can be maintained by any kind of food but cow's milk is required to develop higher faculties of introspection. Human beings are meant to enquire about the meaning of life and that requires finer brain tissues.

In Vedic system, knowledge is divided in two categories - material and spiritual. Material knowledge relates to this body and physical world. Practically all the knowledge imparted in universities and all the scientific research comes in this category. Spiritual knowledge deals with the subject of spirit soul and Super Soul. Spirit soul is the active principle within the body and a part and parcel of God. Spiritual knowledge deals in incorporeal or metaphysical matters and attempts to answer subtle questions on life and universe. Who am I, where do I come from, what is the purpose of life, what happens after death, why is this world created, who is the creator and what is my relationship with Him, is there any other reality, these are some of the questions.

Real knowledge means to know matter and spirit and the controller

There's nothing like sitting back and talking to your cows.
-Russell Crowe

Yoga for beginners

of both. How to eat, sleep, mate and defend, even animals know this without attending any college. Matter is dead and material knowledge is limited to destructible physical elements.

This is where cow milk comes into picture. Great sages in ancient times survived on dairy along with some fruits and grains. They possessed super brains as is evident from their works.

Srila Prabhupada says, "Nothing was written. Vedas were also not written. They were heard from disciplic succession. The first writing business was done by Vyasadeva. Before that, there was nothing in writing. All Vedic scriptures, they were learned by simply hearing. That's all. The brahmacharis will live by the direction of the spiritual master and hear the class, and they will learn. That's all, no written book, neither there was notebook. Everything was heard by students. There was no need of writing. Therefore this whole Vedic literature is called sruti. Sruti means simply hearing. There was... Even in recent years there was a learned pandita in Calcutta. There were some... In the British days there was some quarrel between two Britishers, and one of them complained to the magistrate, and the magistrate inquired, "Who is your witness?" Then one of them said that "Well, there was nobody else. But there was a pandita. He was worshiping in that bank of the Ganges. So we had some quarrel. He has heard it." So he was called. So he stated that "I do not know what they talked because they were talking in English language, but I can produce what they talked." So he produced the whole thing verbatim, that "He talked like this. He talked like this. He talked like this. He talked like this." Just like record, tape record. Just see. Even some hundred years before, the memory was so sharp. Just like tape recorder, it is recorded. This is mechanical. But by nature we have got such nice brain. Just like we remember so many things of our past life. That is recorded. Actually it is recorded. Everything is recorded. How you are getting this television? Because it is recorded in the atmosphere. It is being simply transferred. Everything is recorded. But we have deteriorated in our even physical condition that we cannot produce the recorded version. So we are making ourself dull, duller, dullest. Just like Sir George Bernard Shaw, he also stated that "You are what you eat." So by eating process, we are making our brain dull. So there is need of nice eating, nice talking, nice thinking, nice behavior. *(Lecture, Srimad-Bhagavatam 1.4.25, Montreal, June 20, 1968)*

Srila Prabhupada adds, "Those who are animal killers, their brain is dull as stone. They cannot understand any thing. Therefore meat-

A society concerned only with manufacturing new cars and new skyscrapers every year and then breaking them to pieces and making new ones — may be technologically advanced, but it is not a human civilization. A human civilization is advanced when its people follow the catur-varnya system, the system of four orders of life. There must be ideal, first-class men to act as advisors, second-class men to act as administrators, third-class men to produce food and protect cows, and fourth-class men who obey the three higher classes of society. One who does not follow the standard system of society should be considered a fifth-class man. A society without Vedic laws and regulations will not be very helpful to humanity. As stated in this verse, dharmam te na param viduh: such a society does not know the aim of life and the highest principle of religion.
-Srila Prabhupada (Srimad Bhagavatam 6.7.13)

eating should be stopped. In order to revive the finer tissues of the brain to understand subtle things, one must give up meat-eating." *(Bhagavad-gita 2.18 - London, August 24, 1973)*

Srila Prabhupada further adds, "The brahmana (a spiritualist) cannot take any other food unless it is made of milk preparation. That develops the finer tissues of the brain. You can understand subtle matters, in philosophy, in spiritual science. Just like in a scientific college, no ordinary man can understand the scientific intricacies. They require some preliminary qualification to enter into the scientific college. They require some preliminary qualification to enter into the law college, in the postgraduate classes. Similarly, to understand the subtle or finer implications of spiritual science, one has to become brahmana (a spiritualist). *(Lecture - Los Angeles, December 4, 1968)*

Seventeenth Chapter of the Gita mentions that persons situated in different modes are attracted to different kinds of food. The Supreme Lord says: "Foods in the mode of goodness increase the duration of life, purify existence, give strength and increase health, happiness and satisfaction. Such foods are juicy and fatty, and they are very conducive to the health of the body. Food that is too bitter, too sour, too salty, too pungent, too dry or too hot causes distress, misery and disease. Such food is very dear to those in the mode of passion. Foods prepared more than three hours before being eaten, which are tasteless, juiceless, decomposing, which have a bad smell, and which consist of remnants and untouchable things, are very dear to those in the mode of darkness." (Bhagavad-gita, 17.8–10)

Cow's association makes society happy, wealthy, healthy, honest, and spiritually advanced. If we really want to cultivate the human spirit, we must have intelligent men of character to guide society. And to assimilate the subtle form of transcendental knowledge, we need sufficient milk and milk preparations to develop our finer brain tissues. Ultimately, we need to protect the cow to derive the highest benefit from this important animal. Our relationship with the cow is not only symbiotic, it is sacred.

The cow symbolizes Earth, the nourisher, the ever-giving kind mother. The cow represents life and the sustenance of life. The cow is so generous, taking nothing but grass and chaff and giving the most valuable of foods in return. It gives milk just as the liberated souls bestow spiritual knowledge. The cow is a symbol of grace and

As the ksatriyas were given charge of the protection of the citizens, vaisyas were given the charge of the protection of animals. Animals are never meant to be killed. Killing of animals is a symptom of barbarian society. For a human being, agricultural produce, fruits and milk are sufficient and compatible foodstuffs. The human society should give more attention to animal protection. -(Srimad Bhagavatam -1.9.26p)

abundance. Veneration for the cow instills in human beings the virtues of gentleness, receptivity and connection with nature.

Many holy books mention milk; Bible contains references to the Land of Milk and Honey. In the Quran, there is a request to wonder on milk as follows: 'And surely in the livestock there is a lesson for you, We give you to drink of that which is in their bellies from the midst of digested food and blood, pure milk palatable for the drinkers.'(16-66). The Ramadan fast is traditionally broken with a glass of milk and dates.

From Cruelty To Kindness - Cow Changed A Heart

(Translated From Go Seva Chamatkar)

During the 1857 Sepoy mutiny in India, a small group of Muslim soldiers assembled in a Delhi street. They were tired and hungry after an intense day of looting and fighting. The leader asked them to go and find some food. A group of 4 brought a pregnant cow, dragging her along. The cow had tears in her eyes. They threw her on the ground, tied legs and began sharpening the knife. Somehow the leader's heart melted at the sight and he scolded them for being too slow, "Give me the knife and arrange for fuel and salt. How do you plan to cook her without that?" Soldiers left the scene to arrange for fuel and salt.

After they left, he patted her and set her free. Before walking away, she looked at him lovingly, with eyes full of gratitude.

Shortly afterwards, they were arrested by the British and sentenced to death by hanging. When the leader's turn came, he was handcuffed, masked and the noose was placed on him. When the platform below was moved, his legs came to rest upon something which felt like two horns. His hanging was attempted three times and everytime he felt two horns stopping his fall. As per the prevailing law, he was released

> *Many times Krishna has repeated, go-raksya. Why He did not say "pig-raksya"? No. He said, go-raksya, because without cows' milk there is no civilization. You will not have nice brain to understand things, simply speculate.*
> *-Srila Prabhupada (Lecture, Srimad Bhagavatam 6.1.21 — Honolulu, May 21, 1976)*

after three failed attempts.

As he came out of the prison, he saw the same cow with a beautiful calf, looking at him lovingly and walking away. Since then he dedicated himself to spreading the glories of cow protection. Throughout his life, he would first offer prayers to a cow and then go and offer his namaz.

Story of Ben and Tina - A Cow Teaches How To Love And Care
Amlwch farm, UK

Farmer Keith Ridgeway and wife Elsie own a farm in Amlwch, UK. This year, one of their ewe (sheep) gave birth to triplets. Triplets are very hard to rear and often one will be rejected by the ewe. One of the newborn triplets was rejected by the mother ewe and was not allowed to come near. The tiny lamb just laid on the ground bleating.

To everyone's surprise, an old cow Tina, farmer's pet, came up to nuzzle the little lamb in the yard. When Tina, the cow saw that Ben had been

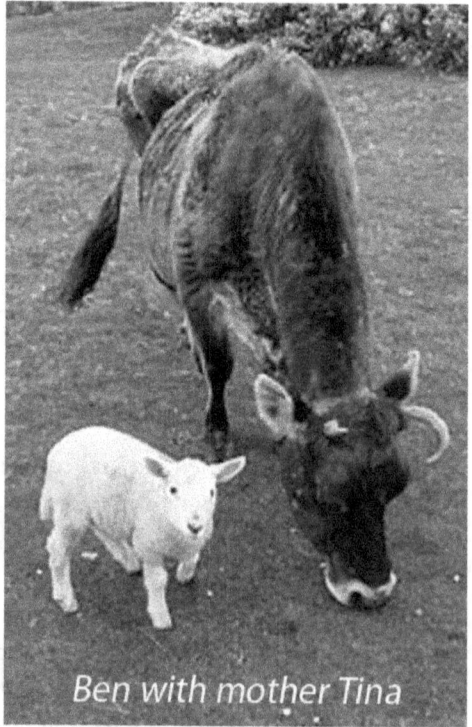

Ben with mother Tina

abandoned, she took him on herself and started playing the role of a mother for him. The lamb has been named 'Ben' since then.

At twenty, Tina is too old for calves now herself, but the mothering instinct in her is very strong. She moos when anyone gets too close to Ben and licks him clean. She really believes she is Ben's mother. Ben just follows her around all over the place and even tries to get milk from her. Tina hasn't produced any milk for about four years so the farmer family has to bottle-feed Ben, but in every other respect, she is now his mother. They even lie down together to sleep.

This benign gesture by the cow has kindled compassion in the farmer Keith and his family's hearts. Keith says, "While the rest of the flock were sold over Easter, Ben's future with Tina is safe. Ben seems to be growing well and the grandchildren like him so much, he will never be served up for dinner. I think Tina and Ben will be friends for the rest of their lives."

Cow Kindles Affectionate Feelings In City Folks

One evening in April 2009, a stray cow delivered a male calf on the streets of Navi Mumbai, India. Mother cow soon left in search of food, leaving the calf in the middle of the road. It was natural for a cow who had just delivered to feel hungry.

The wailing calf attracted the attention of passers by who informed the local branch of Society for the Prevention of Cruelty to Animals and the Navi Mumbai Municipal Corporation (NMMC). SPCA officials soon arrived and brought the calf to SPCA hospital. But, minutes later the cow returned and not finding the calf on the spot she went berserk. She turned violent and started to attack anyone

If we really want to cultivate the human spirit in society we must have first-class intelligent men to guide the society, and to develop the finer tissues of our brains we must assimilate vitamin values from milk. Devotees worship Lord Sri Krsna by addressing Him as the well-wisher of the brahmanas and the cows. The most intelligent class of men, who have perfectly attained knowledge in spiritual values, are called the brahmanas. No society can improve in transcendental knowledge without the guidance of such first-class men, and no brain can assimilate the subtle form of knowledge without fine brain tissues. For such important brain tissues we require a sufficient quantity of milk and milk preparations. Ultimately, we need to protect the cow to derive the highest benefit from this important animal. The protection of cows, therefore, is not merely a religious sentiment but a means to secure the highest benefit for human society.
-Srila Prabhupada (Light of Bhagavata verse 27)

US soldiers in Afghanistan take a break from war and look after a calf

who approached her. For hours together the wailing mother cow searched for her calf all over the area. Calf was not released back on the streets as it would have fallen prey to the butchers.

In the hospital, the calf was wailing for mother and refused to be bottle-fed. SPCA president Shakuntala Majumdar spent several hours that night trying to feed the calf and finally she succeeded. Majumdar laughs, "The moody calf got used to me feeding him and refused to be fed by other staffers. So, even after I left for home, I had to make mooing sounds over the phone so that the calf would have milk. A

Less intelligent people underestimate the value of cow's milk. Cow's milk is also called gorasa, or the juice from the body of the cow. Milk is the most valuable form of gorasa, and from milk we can prepare many important and valuable foodstuffs for the upkeep of the human body. The killing of cows by human society is one of the grossest suicidal policies, and those who are anxious to cultivate the human spirit must turn their attention first toward the question of cow protection.
-Srila Prabhupada (Light of Bhagavata verse 27)

woman staffer even wore my hospital clothes to feed the calf."

Finally, instead of releasing the calf back into the streets, they caught hold of mother cow and brought her to the hospital. It was an emotional reunion, well covered in media. Thus the story ended on a happy note.

This incident moved many locals and many took keen interest in the developments. It touched many hearts. For many, the incident changed their perspective on animals, especially cows. Many felt moved by the wailings of mother cow when it was shown on local television. They never thought animals could have such intense feelings.

Cow Dreams

I've been wonderin' lately,
While I watched some doggies doze
What cows and calves dream about,
and I would suppose,

They dream of lush green pastures,
with clover belly deep.
And rumens full of grass and milk.
But I wonder when they sleep

If they ever dream of mama,
and getting licked so shiney clean.
And of havin' her watching real close by,
and places they have been?

When they are snorin' are they dreamin'
'bout skies of azure blue?
When they have to sleep in snow or rain
I wonder if it's true,

That they have some trouble sleepin'
and wake up with a fright,
From dreams they can't remember,
But bumped loud in the night?

On hot summer days when they are stretched out
takin' a siesta in the shade,
Do you think they dream of autumn
And when dreams begin to fade

When mama tries to wake 'em
to take another lap
To the creek to drink some water,
do they still just want to nap?

And cows that spend their lives in
barns and concrete lots,
Do they dream of dirt and trees and hills,
and shady, grassy spots?

So in retrospect, I reckon,
and there is no shame,
In admittin' that cow's and cowboy's dreams
Are pretty much the same.

-By Steve Lucas

5.

Cow
A Source Of Auspicious Qualities In Human Society

It's no accident that human beings exhibit personalities that resemble animals. People subconsciously modulate their behaviors because each of us have an animal in us. We are an advanced species of animals, albeit bit more polished.

In the animal kingdom, different animals display different personality traits. Some are docile, some are vicious while some are friendly or hostile.

Cow displays some very interesting personality traits. She is considered sacred in vedic tradition for very good reasons. Her good qualities are those that we can emulate.

Cow And Development of Human Qualities

Serene by temperament, herbivorous by diet, the very appearance of a white cow evokes a sense of piety. Vedic authorities strictly forbid cow killing; for compulsive meat eaters, they advise substituting some

All the really good ideas I ever had came to me while I was milking a cow. ~ Grant Wood

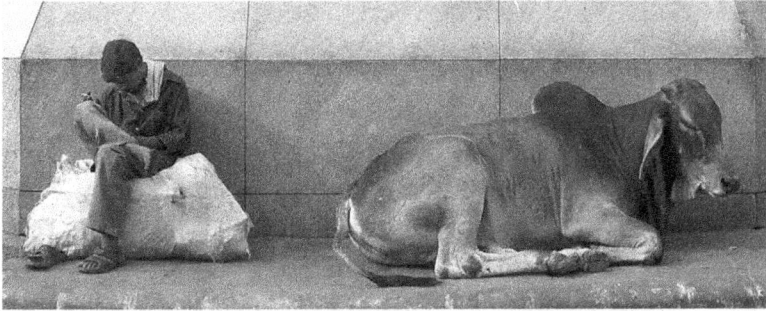

"The time will come when men will look on the murder of animals as they now look on the murder of men."
~Leonardo da Vinci

less important animal instead. Cow protection is thus imperative, for cow's milk stimulates the growth of healthy brain tissues.

Auspicious Human Qualities And Cow Protection

Peacefulness

Almost universally, cows are seen as an emblem of peace. Even the word "bucolic," referring to a peaceful pastoral scene, comes from the Greek word boukolos, which means "cowherd." Unlike dogs and cats, cows are generally not inclined to fight one another, even for food. They are sociable and fond of one another and affectionate to their caretakers. Because cows are naturally peaceful, cowherds tend to take on this quality.

Furthermore, one must have a peaceful demeanor for milking cows and training oxen. Cows and bulls are sensitive to human moods. Cows will not give milk if the milker acts upset. Oxen will not learn commands if the trainer is angry. The cowherd has to cultivate peacefulness to get the job done.

Self-control

To deal effectively with cows and bulls, a keeper has to have patience and forbearance. These animals lead a life at their own pace and can

"Mankind has a free will; but it is free to milk cows and to build houses, nothing more."
~Martin Luther

not be hurried. A farmer has to check his nature, whatever that may be to suit the animals' and adapt to their temperament. Otherwise cows will not be happy. Happy cows means happy farmers and crabby cows lead to broke farmers.

In traditional pastoral communities, crime and host of other social evils are almost nonexistent.

One important aspect of self-control is control of the tongue. When by caring for cows a person sees how friendly and loving they are, his compassionate nature may get aroused. Then he can easily give up eating meat, not wanting to kill the animals he loves and depends on.

Training oxen is another important aid to sense control. There's a New England saying that you train the boy by having him train a team of oxen. There's truth in that. In Sanskrit 'go' means "cow," and it also means "senses." A trainer can see that when the oxen (go) do whatever they feel like, they're useless. Once they're trained and controlled, they're useful and happier. The trainer can see that the oxen are proud and happy to work with him when they can control their senses. The comparison with his own senses (go) is automatic. The trainer sees that when he trains and controls his own senses to serve God, he too will be happier and more productive.

The bull is the emblem of the moral principle, and the cow is the representative of the earth. When the bull and the cow are in a joyful mood, it is to be understood that the people of the world are also in a joyful mood. The reason is that the bull helps production of grains in the agricultural field, and the cow delivers milk, the miracle of aggregate food values. The human society, therefore, maintains these two important animals very carefully so that they can wander everywhere in cheerfulness. But at the present moment in this age of Kali both the bull and the cow are now being slaughtered and eaten up as foodstuff by a class of men who do not know the brahminical culture. .....By advancement of such culture, the morale of society is properly maintained, and so peace and prosperity are also attained without extraneous effort.
(Srimad Bhagavatam 1.16.18)

In Vedic system, one is supposed to offer foods (vegetarian only!) to God or Krishna first before eating them. This spiritual practice of eating offered food promotes control of the tongue. When the cowherd offers Krishna milk products from Krishna's own cows, and grains and vegetables from His own land, and then takes the remnants in the form of prasadam (mercy), the cowherd's brain becomes spiritually purified, and the words he speaks become sober and happy in glorification of God or Krishna.

Austerity

In a society that truly practices cow protection, the bull is fully used for growing food and transporting it. As a valuable member of society, the ox is carefully maintained and protected from slaughter. Economically, using the ox as the means of transport rules out the pileups of wealth that go with trucking things around with coal, gasoline, and nuclear power. Each farmer can farm only so much land with oxen, much less even than with horses. So the use of oxen regulates the scale of production, which helps guarantee that land and wealth are fairly distributed. Economic inequality and social unrest is prevented. There are no 1000-acre agribusinesses. And no heaps of wealth to make it easy for people to become entangled in frivolous activities of sense gratification.

Because the work of caring for the cows and the land is satisfying, artificial sources of pleasure are not required. As spiritual life develops, austerity and simple living become a pleasure, not a burden. A cowherd farmer may not have time and may not feel the need for

Such nice foodstuff. And mostly they are made of milk. These people, they do not know. They kill the cows and throw the milk away to the hogs. And they are proud of their civilization. Like jackals and vultures. Actually, Krishna consciousness movement will transform these uncivilized men to real civilization. Their civilization is now compact in masonry work, collecting stones and bricks and piling them. This much, their civilization. (Room Conversation, June 11, 1974, Paris)

night clubs, bars, cinemas and casinos. Herding the cows and taking care of them day and night engages him or her fully and it is a very satisfying chore.

Purity

Cows can tolerate a wide range of physical conditions. They thrive in the cold Scandinavian countries, in the hot, dry African plains, in the wet tropical jungles of Latin America. But they cannot tolerate filth. They quickly become diseased if not kept clean. As the cowherd works to keep the cows clean, he or she practices living a clean way of life.

Tolerance

Probably no other animal is as tolerant as a cow. If by your daily care and affection you convince the cow or ox that you are its well-wisher, it won't hold a grudge against you for reprimanding it. It won't attack you. For example, once, by my foolish negligence, one of our milk cows got loose from her stall, and when I walked into the barn I found her eating from a grain cart. I knew she could die from overeating if she didn't stop. So I yelled at her, but she didn't stop. I hit her on the back with a stick, but she still kept eating. Finally, I had to hit her in the face, which I hated to do, especially since it was

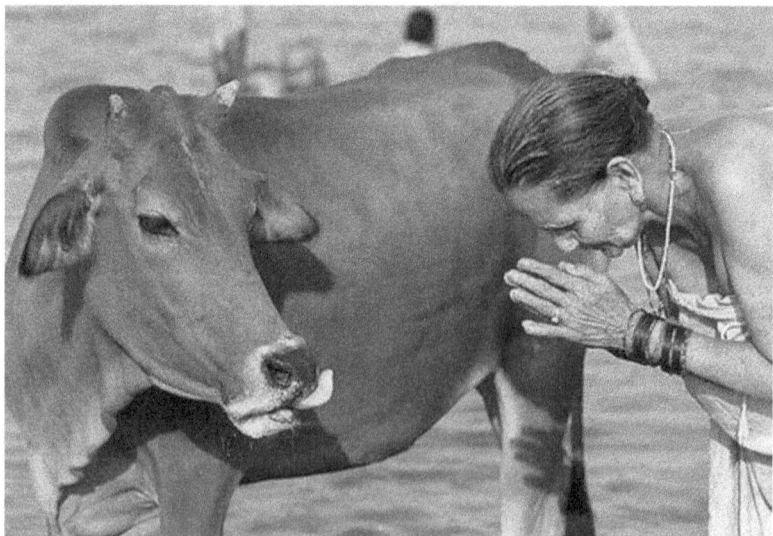

my fault she got loose. But she stopped eating grain and returned to her stall. In five minutes she was mooing softly for me to come and pet her. She wasn't at all afraid of me, and she wasn't angry at me. I knew a dog or cat or even a child would never have such tolerance.

Cows have very high threshold for pain tolerance. They do not reveal their ailments so easily. But a person they trust can find out about their health issues more easily than a stranger. When in pain or heading for slaughter, pigs squeal and thrash around but cows tolerate it very soberly. The cowherd can learn tolerance from the cows and oxen.

Honesty

Cows are straightforward, and their service demands straightforwardness. It's hard to cheat with them. Either you give them good food, water, and affection or you don't. Either you are punctual for milkings or you're not. Either you keep them clean or you don't. When you make a mistake or get lazy, you'll probably get a quick reaction. You're too lazy to clean out the water tank? Milk production will drop because cows don't want to drink that nasty-tasting water. You forgot about the six o'clock milking? You'll be

Human society without brahminical culture is animal society. We offer our obeisances to the Lord, namo brahmanya-devaya go-brahmana-hitaya ca. Krsna is first of all interested to see whether in the society the brahmana and the cow is properly respected. Namo brahmanya-devaya go-brahmana-hitaya ca. His first business is to see that the brahmana and cow is being properly honored. Then jagad-dhitaya. Then automatically the whole world will be peaceful. This secret of success they do not know. Nobody is prepared to become brahmana, and so far cow protection is concerned, it is in the oblivion. This is the whole world position. Therefore it is in chaotic condition. It must be, because this is animal society. When these two things are neglected, it is animal society, and then other animal qualities and paraphernalia follow.
-Srila Prabhupada (Lecture, Srimad-Bhagavatam 5.5.23, Vrndavana, November 10, 1976)

kicking yourself tomorrow when you have to take care of a cow suffering from mastitis. You'll probably never forget again. Cow protection is a practical way of learning to be honest and conscientious.

Knowledge And Wisdom

Cultivation of spiritual knowledge starts with a healthy brain. For this, milk is essential. Prabhupada explains, "The body can be maintained by any kind of foodstuff, but cow's milk is particularly essential for developing the finer tissues of the human brain so that one can understand the intricacies of transcendental knowledge." (Srimad-Bhagavatam 3.5.7)

Scientists support this view. They say that Vitamin B12 is essential to maintain healthy nerve cells. (The brain is made up of nerve cells.) A Vitamin-B12 deficiency can take years to manifest, but it is a deadly serious matter, as explained by nutrition expert Laurel Roberts. "The first signs of damage are a characteristic sore back, numbness and tingling in the feet, and diminished vibration and position sense. Then follow unsteadiness, poor memory, confusion, moodiness, delusions, overt psychosis, and eventually death."

The only natural source of vitamin B12 in a vegetarian diet is milk. (Obtaining B12 from meat products creates new problems because of the adrenalin and toxins one ingests with the meat.) In a peaceful society, therefore, milk is essential to properly maintain brain cells needed for spiritual intelligence. Prabhupada emphasizes this point again, "For such important brain tissues we require a sufficient quantity of milk and milk preparations. Ultimately, we need to protect the cow to derive the highest benefit from this important animal. The protection of cows, therefore, is not merely a religious sentiment but a means to secure the highest benefit for human society." (Light of the Bhagavata)

Thus when the cowherd comes home and takes a cup of hot milk at the end of a day of hard work in the fields, he or she is making the brain fit to contemplate spiritual topics. And the peaceful fields and pastures provide the perfect environment to cultivate knowledge and wisdom.

Religiousness

No need to be a great scholar. No need to be a powerful warrior, or even a highly talented craftsman. If the cowherd faithfully carries out the duties of caring for the cows and bulls and producing food to offer to God, he or she will become spiritually satisfied.

"Milk is liquid religiosity," says Srila Prabhupada. So what could be more religious than to produce milk and grains and offer them to God? Bhagavad-gita says that a person can understand God only by devotional service. (Bg. 18.55) And one can perform devotional service by doing one's daily work as an offering to God (Bg. 18. 45,46). Besides that, just by seeing the cows every day one can easily remember Krishna and His cows in Goloka Vrindavan, in the spiritual sky. That remembrance is the highest religiousness.

Through philosophy and scripture alone a few intelligent people can be motivated to undertake spiritual life. For them to get started on the path back to Godhead may be easy. But most of us are not like that. For us God has very kindly sent the cow and the bull to coach us in developing qualities that will help us in God consciousness.

In a plush cloth showroom in India, a street bull likes to sit around while the business goes on as usual.

Warmth And Personalism

In today's 'me and mine' civilization, people have become impersonal. Isolation and urban loneliness are emerging as major issues of the day. Modern man is utterly lonely amidst the swarming city crowds. Man is trying to explore moon but has no idea about the next door neighbor.

Pastoral life, surrounded by cows and bulls is different. There is bound to be intimate exchange and community feelings between humans and between animals and humans. Amidst these loving creatures, there is no chance of becoming lonely. Cows expect very personal dealings and want to be called by a name.

In fact a study by the university's School of Agriculture, Food and Rural Development, involving 516 farmers across the UK, found that cows that are named and treated with a "more personal touch" can increase milk yields by up to 500 pints a year. The study, Published in the journal Anthrozoos, found farmers who named their cows gained a higher yield than the 54% that did not give their cattle names. Dairy farmer Dennis Gibb, who co-owns Eachwick Red House Farm outside Newcastle with his brother Richard, said he believed treating every cow as an individual was "vitally important".

Thus Cow protection contains valuable lessons on how to be warm and personal.

(By Mataji Hare Krishna Dasi, slightly edited.)

Cow In Vedas

वन्दनीयाश्च पूज्याश्च गाव: सेव्यास्तु नित्यश:।
गवां गोष्ठे स्थितानां तु य: करोति प्रदक्षिणम्। प्रदक्षिणीकृतं तेन जगत् सदसदात्मकम्॥
शृङ्गोदकं गवां पुण्यं सर्वाघविनिषूदनम्। गवां कण्डूयनं चैव सर्वकल्मषनाशनम्॥
गवां ग्रासप्रदानेन स्वर्गलोके महीयते।
लवणं च यथाशक्त्या गवां ये वै ददन्ति च। तेषां पुण्यकृतां लोका गवां लोकं व्रजन्ति ते॥
योऽग्रं भक्त्या किंचिदप्यश्य दद्याद् गोभ्यो नित्यं गोव्रती सत्यवादी।
शान्तो बुद्धो गोसहस्रस्य पुण्यं संवत्सरेणाप्नुयाद्धर्मशील:॥
गोकुलस्य तृषार्तस्य जलान्ते वसुधाधिप। उत्पादयति यो विघ्नं तमाहुर्ब्रह्मघातकम्॥
कृत्वा गवार्थे शरणं शीतवातक्षर्मं महत्। आसन्नमर्मं तारयति कुलं भरतसत्तम॥
मनुष्यैस्तृणतोयाद्यैर्गाव: पाल्या: प्रयत्नत:। देवा: पूज्याश्च पोष्याश्च प्रतिपाल्याश्च सर्वदा॥
घासग्रासादिकं देयं निशि दीप: सुभास्वर:। इतिहासपुराणानां व्याख्यानं सोपवीजनम्॥
अन्तस्तुष्ट्यर्थयाशक्त्या परिचर्या यथाक्रमम्। ताडनाक्रोशखेदाश्च स्वप्नेऽपि न कदाचन॥
तासां मूत्रपुरीषे तु नोद्वेग: क्रियते क्वचित्। शोधनीयश्च गोवाट: शुष्कक्षारादिकै: सदा॥
ग्रीष्मे वृक्षाकुले वेश्म शीततोये विकर्दमे। वर्षासु चाथ शिशिरे सुखोष्णे वातवर्जिते॥
उच्छिष्टं मूत्रविद्श्लेष्ममलं जह्यान्न तत्र च। रजस्वला न प्रवेश्या नान्त्यजातिर्न पुंश्चली॥
न लङ्घयेद्वत्सतरीं न क्रीडेद्रोष्ठसंनिधौ। न गन्तव्यं गवां मध्ये सोपानत्कै: सपादुकै:॥
हस्त्यश्वरथयानैश्च सवितानै: कदाचन। दक्षिणोत्तरगै: प्रह्वैर्गन्तव्यं च पदातिभि:॥
गाव: कृशातुरा: पाल्या: श्रद्धया पितृमातृवत्।

Cows should always be offered respects, worshiped and served.

One who circumambulates the cows in a cowshed, he achieves the result of circumambulating all the universes, both ephemeral and eternal.

Water that has washed a cow's horns, is supremely pure and destroys all sinful reactions of a living entity. Scratching and massaging mother cow's body washes off all sins and contaminations in the heart.

One who feeds the cows, achieves heavenly planets and is glorified there.

If someone offers cows salt, according to one's capacity, he ascends to the planets of the pious living entities and then proceeds to Goloka, the spiritual kingdom.

A Person who is truthful, peaceful and devoted to cows, if he feeds the cows everyday for one year before eating anything, such person becomes very learned and achieves the result of donating one thousand cows.

One who prevents thirsty and tired cows from drinking water from a pond, that sinful person accrues the sin of killing a brahmin and is known as a killer of a brahmin.

A person who constructs a cowshed to shelter cows from heat, cold, wind and rain, delivers seven generations of his ancestors.

Somehow, every person should maintain cows by feeding them straw and grass. Cows always deserve to be maintained, worshiped and given in charity.

Feeding mother cow should always be done carefully. In the evenings, a cowshed should be illuminated with bright lamps. Cows should be fanned and narrations from histories and Puranas should be recited to them.

One should serve cows wholeheartedly and with great pleasure according to one's capacity. Such service should be regulated and punctual. Even in dreams, one should not hurt a cow, get angry or misbehave with her.

Cows should not be disturbed while answering a call of nature and a cowshed should be kept very clean by brooming etc.

In summer a cowshed should be under the shade of trees and near cool water bodies In rainy season it should be free from muddiness and in winter, the cowshed should be comfortably warm and protected from chilly winds.

A cowshed or area around it should never be defiled by leftovers from a plate, urine, excrement or spit etc. A woman in periods, a low class woman and a woman of shady character should not be allowed to enter therein.

A calf or a rope tying such a calf should never be stepped over or crossed over. In and around cowshed, there should be no playing or sporting.

One should not go amidst cows with slippers or shoes on, neither should one enter a cowshed riding a horses or elephant. Also entering a cowshed in a vehicle or palanquin or with a ceremonial umbrella cover is prohibited. A person should walk to cows, keeping them always on the right side.

Cows that are sick or suffering from hunger and thirst, cows that are lean and thin or in distress, should be served with care and attention. They should be treated just like one's mother and father and should never be neglected in anyway.

Q: Why do cows wear cow bells?
A: Because their horns don't work.

6.

Ungrateful Humanity

Hoping Against Hope To Live In Peace

There is a connection between cruelty towards animals and wars in human society. Animal slaughter and violence in human society are interrelated. 20th century saw the establishment of global networks in animal products and inhumane factory farming system. At the same time, 20th century also saw the two most brutal World Wars, the worst acts of barbarism like holocaust, Gulag concentration camps, genocides and atomic bombing of Hiroshima and Nagasaki. It was the bloodiest century in human history. This is what Mahatma Gandhi meant by his saying, *"Cow-slaughter and man-slaughter are in my opinion the two sides of the same coin."* The same sentiments were echoed by George Bernard Shaw, *"The Peace we say we are anxious for? Thus cruelty begets its offspring—War."*

It is not a question of religion, ritual or philosophy. We are talking common sense here. What right do we have to butcher poor animals and especially ones like cows who render such valuable service. Now if you say, it is natural to eat flesh, animals all around us kill other animals, then the Roman author Plutarch has a challenge for you, "If you declare that you are naturally designed for such a diet, then first kill for yourself what you want to eat. Do it, however, only through your own resources, unaided by cleaver or cudgel or any kind of ax."

In an essay titled "On Eating Flesh," he continues "Can you really ask what reason Pythagoras had for abstinence from flesh? For my part I rather wonder both by what accident and in what state of mind the first man touched his mouth to gore and brought his lips to the flesh of a dead creature, set forth tables of dead, stale bodies, and ventured to call food and nourishment the parts that had a little before bellowed and cried, moved and lived. How could eyes endure the slaughter when throats were slit and hides flayed and limbs torn from limb? How could his nose endure the stench? How was it that the pollution did not turn away his taste, which made contact with sores of others and sucked juices and serums from mortal wounds? It is certainly not lions or wolves that we eat out of self-defense; on the contrary, we ignore these and slaughter harmless, tame creatures without stings or teeth to harm us. For the sake of a little flesh we deprive them of sun, of light, of the duration of life to which they are entitled by birth and being."

"Why should man expect his prayer for mercy to be heard by What is above him when he shows no mercy to what is under him?", asks Pierre Troubetzkoy

You Can Talk of Peace Till the Cows Come Home
An inside look at the link between cow slaughter and war.
by His Grace Suresvara dasa
Winter is again upon us, and again the world staggers through its

Now if you are willingly killing cows and so many animals, so how much you are being responsible? Therefore at the present moment there is war, and the human society becomes subjected to be killed in mass massacre -- the nature's law. You cannot stop war and go on killing animals. That is not possible. There will be so many accidents for killing. The wholesale kill. When Krsna kills, He kills wholesale. When I kill -- one after another. But when Krsna kills, they assemble all the killers and kill. -Srila Prabhupada (Srimad-Bhagavatam 6.1.8-13 -- New York, July 24, 1971)

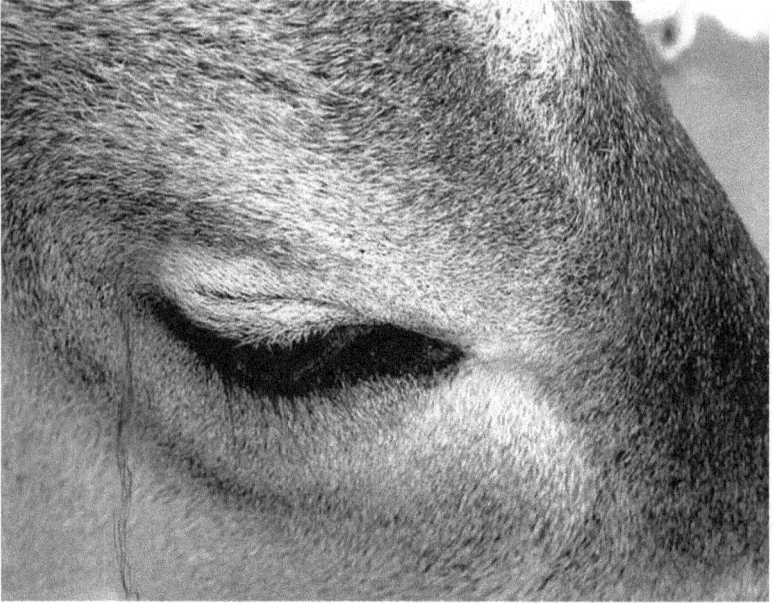

holy days, raging with quarrel and war. And though we know winter will soon leave us, when, we wonder, will war?

To answer, let's go back some fifty centuries to ancient India, where a white cow and bull are grazing peacefully on the shore of the Sarasvati River. Suddenly, out of the tall grasses, a swarthy, bearded man appears, brandishing a club. He wears the dress of royalty, but when he attacks the innocent cow and bull, he shows himself to be a low-class rogue.

Then the real king appears - Maharaja Pariksit. With sword upraised, Pariksit addresses the man, with a voice like thunder.

"You rogue, how dare you beat an innocent cow just because Lord Krsna is no longer present? You are a culprit and deserve to be killed!"

Just like we are taking milk from the cow. We are indebted. "No, we are killing them." They are committing simply sinful life and they want to be happy and peaceful. Just see. We are i indebted. I am obliged to you for your service. So instead of feeling obligation, if I cut your throat, how gentleman I am, just see, imagine.
-Srila Prabhupada (Bhagavad-gita 1.37-39, London, July 27, 1973)

Fearing for his life, the man, named Kali, gives up his royal dress and begs the king's mercy. Pariksit spares the mischievous Kali, then banishes him to places of gambling, drinking, prostitution, animal slaughter, and hoarding of gold.

This Kali-Pariksit encounter marked the dawn of what Vedic historians call the Age of Kali, our present age of quarrel and hypocrisy. The Supreme Lord Krsna had just left the earth, and Pariksit was determined to protect the universal religious principles the Lord had revived during His visit. But Kali was just as determined to raise hell; and inexorable time was on his side. As winter follows autumn, so Kali follows Krsna, and the best Pariksit could do was temporarily contain him. Places of gambling, drinking, prostitution, and animal slaughter didn't exist in pious Pariksit's day, but when Kali found gold, he was in business. And so was our age.

Our Age of Kali has come a long way since the first attempt to kill a cow and bull. Gambling, drinking, prostitution, and animal slaughter are big business now, often sanctioned and taxed by the government. Kali's spirit possesses us. Excessive pride has ruined our self-control, and excessive sex our health. Intoxication has destroyed our mercy, lying has obscured the truth, and peace has given way to war.

Kali's spirit of quarrel and hypocrisy pervades even religion, whose mere lip-servers repulse as many as they attract and give God a bad name. Even before church picnics, hayrides, and bingo parties introduce many of us to drinking, sex, and gambling, Kali confirms us as meat-eaters by serving us the flesh of cows. How often have we drunk the cow's milk with one hand and eaten her flesh with the other?

"One who, being fully satisfied by milk, is desirous of killing the cow, is in the grossest ignorance," writes Srila Prabhupada, the founder

"There exists no politician in India daring enough to attempt to explain to the masses that cows can be eaten." - Indira Gandhi (former Indian Prime Minister, while speaking in favour of cow killing.)

and spiritual guide of the Hare Krsna movement. "We drink cows' milk; therefore the cow is our mother. And Lord Krsna has created the bull to produce grains for our maintenance; therefore he is our father. Since the bull and cow are our father and mother, how can we kill and eat them? What kind of civilization is this?"

The simple truth of this challenge is lost to most of us. Recently, the American Dairy Association awarded McDonald's, the world's largest restaurant organization, the use of its "REAL" seal, which helps customers distinguish dairy foods from imitations. But Lord Krsna's instructions in the Bhagavad-gita to protect the cow expose the A.D.A. as an imitation dairy association. Why? Because along with an annual 120 million cartons of real milk, 380 million real milk shakes, and 300 million soft-serve ice cream cones and sundaes, McDonald's has handled enough real cow's flesh over the years to sell upwards of 45 billion hamburgers. In other words, instead of protecting the cow, Kali's dairyman is in cahoots with the slaughterhouse.

if you kill me my mommy will be sad

It is ignorance that compels us to slaughter from 35 to 40 million cows a year. When we buy the nicely-wrapped meat in the market, we have no idea of the suffering we are bringing ourselves by this act. Srila Prabhupada explains:

In this Age of Kali, the propensity for mercy is almost nil. Consequently, there is always fighting and wars between men and nations. Men do not understand that because they unrestrictedly kill so many animals, they also must be slaughtered like animals in big wars. Sometimes during war, soldiers keep their enemies in concentration camps and kill them in very cruel ways. These are reactions brought about by unrestricted animal-killing in the slaughterhouse. As long as human society continues to allow cows to be regularly killed in slaughterhouses, there cannot be any question of peace and prosperity.

Of course, there's always hope for peace, just as, during the bleakest winter, there's still the chance of a sunny day. Kali's clouds of ignorance, thick as they are, cannot yet deny us the truth -- when we see it. And so with this in mind, I would like to tell you about my recent visit to a slaughterhouse.

The pictures on the walls told a story of which Kali must be proud. Around the turn of the century, the founder ran a one-man butchering business. He slaughtered several animals weekly and sold his meat

But we want to stop these killing houses. It is very, very sinful. Therefore in Europe, so many wars. Every ten years, fifteen years, there is a big war and wholesale slaughter of the whole human kind. And these rascals, they do not see it. The reaction must be there. You are killing innocent cows and animals. Nature will take revenge. Wait for that. As soon as the time is ripe, the nature will gather all these rascals, and club, slaughter them. Finished. They will fight amongst themselves, Protestant and Catholic, Russian and France, and France and Germany. This is going on. Why? This is the nature's law. Tit for tat. You have killed. Now you become killed. Amongst yourselves. They are being sent to the slaughterhouse. And here, you'll create slaughterhouse, "Dum! dum!" and be killed. -Srila Prabhupada (Room Conversation -- June 11, 1974, Paris)

products from a horse-drawn wagon. Then times started to change. Refrigeration, mechanization, the automobile, and two of the founder's sons brought growth to the business. Soon, founder and sons were slaughtering 125 cows weekly, then daily, as they kept gaining more customers and adding more employees and equipment. Over the years, steady growth brought the "packing company" to its present position as the "largest beef slaughterer and fabricator" in the eastern United States.

Kali is so well established that now the king's men federally inspect and grade his slaughtered cows. And for those who can take it, he gives tours.

Rose, my guide, was fortyish, frowsy, and fat as a heifer. Wearing hard hats and smocks we walked out onto a catwalk overlooking the holding pens. A thousand cows bellowed beneath us. The ammonia in the air almost covered the smell of death nearby. Although Rose sounded a little like Dale Evans when she spoke, she sounded even more like the Queen of Hearts.

"We slaughter steers, heifers, and cows -- about 1,300 a day. Would you like to see the stunning?" I nodded, walked through a doorway, and suddenly beheld the most ghastly scene imaginable.

Pistol shots. Cows and bulls upside down. Blood everywhere. What the devil's going on? I looked where Rose was pointing. A man walked over to a Holstein bound to a conveyor, jammed a gun into her forehead, and fired.

"The stunner fires a sliding bolt into the animal's brain," Rose yelled above the din. "Then it's shackled and hoisted -- still alive but insensible to pain. The butcher down there finishes the job by severing the major arteries with a six-inch double-edge sticking knife."

Because people in Kali-yuga are mandah, all bad, and sumanda-matayah, misled by false conceptions of life, they are killing cows in the thousands. Therefore they are unfortunate in spiritual consciousness, and nature disturbs them in so many ways, especially through incurable diseases like cancer and through frequent wars and among nations. As long as human society continues to allow cows to be regularly killed in slaughterhouses, there cannot be any question of peace and prosperity.
-Srila Prabhupada (SB 8.8.11)

World leaders At G8 Summit. Talking of peace with dead cows in their bellies.

Tongue hanging, eyes bulging, the Holstein rose in the air, kicking and thrashing in her shackle -- obviously fighting for life. Her udder began to spurt milk.

"Just a nervous reaction," Rose assured me. "The body is 'brain dead.'"

The body? What about the struggling soul? What about the progressive journey of all souls back to Godhead? And what about the Supreme Personality of Godhead Himself, Lord Krsna, the soul-

The cow is not my mother? Who can live without milk? And who has not taken cow's milk? Immediately, in the morning, you require milk. And the animal, she's supplying milk, she's not mother? What is the sense? Mother-killing civilization. And they want to be happy. And periodically there is great war and wholesale massacre, reaction.
-Srila Prabhupada (Garden Conversation, June 14, 1976, Detroit)

ll0

giving father of all species?

But Kali runs his religions the same way he runs his wars. Cows and bulls, like enemies, have no souls. They're subhuman, nonpersons. Kill them.

The stunner, his eyes black pools under a white hard hat, reloaded his pistol. He and the butcher were killing better than a hundred cows an hour and, according to Vedic literature, preparing a dark future for themselves: "Cow killers are condemned to rot in hellish life for as many thousands of years as there are hairs on the body of the cow." But there was no need to tell anyone here they were going to hell. Awash with blood, the "Kill Floor" made the Bible's lake of fire look like Palm Springs.

It was hard for me to keep talking to Rose as though everything was all right. Kali's men held big knives, and Maharaja Pariksit was nowhere in sight. As we walked through blood puddles, my only sword was a pen.

"After the kill, the animals are dehided by a stripper, eviscerated, split into sides, weighed, and shrouded for chilling in the coolers."

Nazi and Soviet death camps never enjoyed such efficiency or such good public relations. And why not? The public's dinner table is the last stop on the production line.

"You have just dined," wrote Emerson, "and however scrupulously the slaughterhouse is concealed in the graceful distance of miles, there is complicity."

We passed into the "Fabrication Plant," where workers boned and trimmed the meat for packaging. Their faces showed many different

The Supreme Personality of Godhead has instructed in Bhagavad-gita (18.44), krsi-go-raksya-vanijyam vaisya-karma-svabhavajam: "Farming, cow protection and trade are the qualities of work for the vaisyas." Nanda Maharaja belonged to the vaisya community, the agriculturalist community. How to protect the cows and how rich this community was are explained in these verses. We can hardly imagine that cows, bulls and calves could be cared for so nicely and decorated so well with cloths and valuable golden ornaments. How happy they were. ~Srila Prabhupada (Srimad Bhagavatam 10.5.7p)

extractions, a kind of General Assembly of butchers. I thought of the United Nations, of how its buildings stand on the very spot where New York City slaughterhouses used to, and of how its members have failed to keep the peace.

A prime example is the Middle East, where destiny has embroiled Christians, Moslems, and Jews -- the world's "religious" meat-eaters -- in a perennial paradigm of hatred and war. The peoples to whom the Lord delivered the Old Testament, New Testament, and Koran are always reinterpreting His words to suit their appetites. Now, "Thou shall not kill," conveniently reads, "Thou shall not commit murder," and the Moslem's and the Jew's "ritual slaughter" of fully conscious cows turns out to be more cruel than the "humane" stun-killing of the Christian. But the Lord is pleased with neither. And war in the Middle East -- and everywhere else -- continues.

Watching mother cow and father bull become man's meat -- horrible as it was -- left no doubt about the connection between slaughter and war. The misapplied technology that increased the slaughter in the founder's "packing company" also increased the slaughter in World Wars 1 and II. And the dues owed since then are in the billions.

Back home from the slaughterhouse, I walked among our Hare Krsna farm's Brown Swiss cows and bulls, who welcomed me with licks and nudges. We looked up as a military jet thundered across the sky. Even if an atomic war doesn't come, I reflected, only Krsna

All the people who are less than the sudras. They are called pancamas, fifth grade. First grade, brahmana, second grade, ksatriya, third grade, vaisya, fourth grade, sudra, and all others -- fifth grade. They are called candalas. The candalas... The sweeper, the cobbler, and the... Low grade. Still, in India, these fifth-grade persons only, they eat meat, pigs, and sometimes cows. Fifth grade. Now it has become a practice. And he's a first-grade man. So just see. What was the business of the fifth-grade men, that has become the business of the so-called politicians. You see. So if you are ruled by the fifth-grade men, then how you can be happy? That is not possible. How there can be any social tranquillity? That is not possible. -Srila Prabhupada (Lecture, Srimad-Bhagavatam 1.5.23, Vrndavana, August 4, 1974) consciousness can release us from the slaughterhouse of repeated birth and death. And if enough of us become Krsna conscious, then even communists and capitalists can learn how to protect cows and live peacefully during Kali's wintry age of discontent.

Universal Love, Brotherhood, Equality, Liberty And Fraternity - Mere High Sounding Words

Universal love, brotherhood, equality, liberty and fraternity - these are mere high sounding words. When an innocent animal is butchered, where is universal love or brotherhood? Where is equality or liberty when billions of animals undergo harrowing suffering. Where is fraternity for millions of animals, being experimented upon in hellish laboratories. Is this not terrorism? Why those complicit in such horrific crimes - farmers, butchers, supermarkets, restaurants, cooks and meateaters, are not listed as terrorists. What is the big difference between having two legs and four legs? What is so great about having two legs and what is so wrong with having four legs? What right these two-legged animals have over four-legged animals to inflict so much pain. Aren't these four legged animals more humane and more warmhearted? Do the four-legged animals ever rob, lie, cheat, rape, drop atom bombs and kill babies in the womb? Do four-legged animals ever indulge in arson, bribery, burglary and child abuse? Did any one hear of them doing pornography, credit card fraud, domestic violence or drug trafficking? Where are the hate crimes, extortion, kidnapping, prostitution or racketeering in animal kingdom? And do they ever seek enjoyment in others suffering?

Who is more human of the two? Where is the humanity in the

So we have created a society for killing cows and eating the meat and maintaining slaughterhouse in the name of religion. This is going on. So how we can be happy? There cannot be happiness. It is not a sentiment. Therefore this is most sinful activity, meat-eating, cow killing. Most sinful activity. And you have to suffer for that. Unfortunately, these rascals, they do not know that what is the result of this sinful activity. -Srila Prabhupada (Lecture, Srimad-Bhagavatam 1.10.4 -- London, November 25, 1973)

two-legged animals? Why is the term 'human' being misused and misapplied on these two legged animals? What have these two-legged animals achieved in all these years other than destroying the planet, destroying

This picture may be an insult. Whether to the person on the left or to the person on the right, depends on your perspective.

life and destroying their ownselves. Shouldn't they take lessons from these honest and unpretentious creatures on how to live, how to behave and how to work.

A cow being tortured to death asks her tormentor, 'What are you good for? I am useful when alive and useful when dead. What is your utility when alive or dead other than giving pain to others. Even my urine and stool are useful. Cow chips are used as a fuel, as a fertilizer. From my skin, shoes are made, apparels and drums are made; does your skin have any value? Even my horns and hooves are put to good use and you don't even have them! Then I give milk for one and all, do you give any? From my milk, butter, cheese, ice cream, yogurt,

There are so many doctrines of universal love, universal friendship, fraternity, but they are fighting, and they are killing simply, because there is no God consciousness. If you are universal, if you are after universal love, then how you can maintain regular slaughterhouse? How you can think that an American gentleman or lady is your countryman and not a cow, and not a goat, not a serpent? Where is your universal idea? So unless there is development of God consciousness, this universal ideas, oh, these are nonsense. There cannot be. It is all false, jugglery of words. So first business is to understand your identity, identity of God, your relationship, and your action reformed in that way. Then there is question of universal, brotherhood, universal...
-Srila Prabhupada (Bhagavad-gita 10.8 — New York, January 6, 1967)

milkshakes are made; is there anything made from yours? One and all like my milk and its good for health; there is no end to my utility and my services to society. And you good for nothing guy, tell me what right you have to torture and kill me?

Appendix

To Further The Cause of Cow Protection
Some Practical Steps

(Some of the following are the excerpts from the Author's earlier book, To Kill Cow Means To End Human Civilization)

The first step in cow protection would be to stop eating them. Of course, in many cultures like Hindus of India, abstaining from beef is already in practice.

Every household can adopt a cow or can feel responsible for the livelihood of a cow. It does not necessarily mean personally taking care but it could be sponsoring a cow in one of the organizations that look after cows.

Traditional Hindus had many interesting practices related to cow protection which one may adapt as far as possible. Many families still continue their tradition in this regard.

In many homes, the first chapati (Indian bread) they cook is kept aside for cows. Since cooking is done at least twice a day, cows get a minimum of two chapatis from each family. The offering to God or saying grace is done with the second chapati. This means the cow's share precedes that of God's. Also vegetable and fruit peels and other leftovers are carefully collected for feeding them. Jaggery and molasses are their favorites and many families keep sufficient stock of these.

On social occasions like childbirth, marriage or bereavement, a portion of expenditure is dedicated towards cow protection. But these days billions of rupees are spent in lavish Hindu ceremonies like marriages but not a penny is spared for this cause. It was a tradition to seek the blessings of cow and bull on these auspicious occasions. When some one in the family fell sick, a cow would be fed and a prayer would be offered for quick recovery. Also water was kept in front of the house for stray cows and other animals and birds.

It was believed that a family would be comfortable if it kept its cows comfortably. A society's well-being was gauged by the well-being of the cows. Vedic literatures mention that an entire family or nation can be doomed if the cows are in distress. If this is true than today's society is unhappy because it has failed in its duty of cow protection.

Also it was common to set aside a certain percentage of income for the cows. Many families even now set aside one rupee a day for this purpose. When famine strikes, some families go out of their way to take care of the cows. It is not uncommon to find skinny human beings and well-fed cows. Traditionally, old cows and bulls were looked after just like old parents, with entire family tending to their needs.

Traditional educational system, taught in the gurukulas, emphasized the importance of cow protection. Today's educational system discusses the benefits of cow slaughter and beef export. India is already a world leader in beef export. Many Brazilian and Australian companies are unable to compete and going bankrupt.

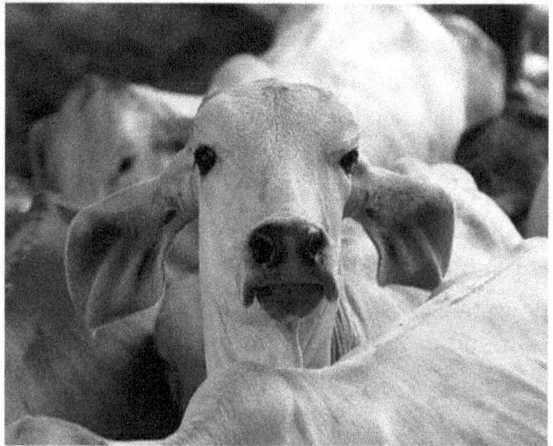

The virtue of kindness has to be inculcated from a tender age. Cow protection needs to be included in the standard curriculum. If Garuda (bird carrier of Lord Vishnu) can be the national symbol of an Islamic country like Indonesia, cow can definitely be the national animal of India. In India, cow protection remains a hotly debated issue. Many organizations are struggling to get cow slaughter completely banned while the government is trying to modernize slaughterhouses and augment beef export earnings.

If cow keeping becomes economically viable, that will immediately stop cow slaughter in India. Farmers often sell their cattle unwillingly out of economic pressure. If people start using cow products like toothpaste, soaps, medicines, fertilizers, pesticides etc., there will be no more cows available for slaughter.

Main utility of cow is her dung and urine. Milk was always considered a byproduct. Today cow's main function is to provide milk and meat.

Leaving aside all cow products, if Indians just take two spoons of cow urine distillate every morning, it will save many cows and health of the nation will improve dramatically. In turn it will save billions in health care. Cow based rural economy is the only way to go for the third world countries like India. That's the only way the village economies can flourish and the masses can rise above the poverty line.

Cow is a mobile dispensary. Over 150 medicines are being manufactured out of cow products now. These medicines, known as 'panchagavya chikitsa' work like a charm.

This is the only viable system of medicine for Indian masses. Modern health care is a failure even in a country like America where it remains

Prabhupada: Now Kirtanananda was prosecuted because he is not killing cows.
Brahmananda: By having them grow old, they were saying that "This is cruelty. You should kill them."
Prabhupada: This is their civilization, that "You are not killing? You are cruel." Just see. Christ said, "Thou shall not kill." That is cruel. How can you pull on this civilization? But this is their religion. So what kind of persons they are?
- Srila Prabhupada (Room Conversation - February 28, 1977, Mayapur)

a hotly debated issue. Health care is a multi-trillion dollar industry with strong muscle and lobbying power. India in next five years is investing $216 billion in health care infrastructure but it will remain out of reach for over 90% of the population. Health care system based on cow products is cheap and effective. It is highly suitable for rural masses who have easy access to cows. Panchagavya centers can be established on village level not only in India but all over the third world.

Now many medical colleges have started courses on panchagavya and dedicated cow science universities (called Kamdhenu visvavidyalaya) are coming up.

Cow is the single fact which can unite numerous factions of Hinduism. No matter what is one's path, every Hindu agrees on the universal practice of cow protection. In Hinduism, different schools of philosophical thought exist and some of them don't see each other eye to eye. But still there is complete agreement on one point - cow protection.

Today's younger generation is blamed for not showing enough

respect to elders. In traditional India, children were taught to respect mother cow and bull from an early age and this training extended to their original parents. As old cows and bulls are slaughtered now, a time will come when old parents would similarly be killed and their organs exported.

Every town and village in India had cow service cooperatives known as pinjarapoles. Retired cows passed their last days there in comfort and dignity. The local communities organized and executed this on a cooperative basis.

No cow should be left to loiter on Indian streets. They lead a very miserable life. Suffering from hunger, thirst and disease, they are often injured by moving vehicles. How can any sane person turn a blind eye to such a pathetic sight. Every town and city should have veterinary hospital for sick and injured cows. *CareforCows.org* is doing a commendable work in this connection in Vraja area of north India. In Delhi and NCR area, *Love4cow Trust* is spearheading the efforts in caring for stray cows. They have a truck with hydraulic system to carry sick or injured cows. Similar facilities are required for every Indian town and city.

Biogas and fertilizer from cow dung represent humanity's future

So this is our program. Let the cows live. We take sufficient milk. We are getting milk, one thousand pounds. One thousand pounds daily in our, one center, New Vrindaban, Virginia. So we are making various preparations from the milk, and they are very happy, and the cows are also happy. So this is one of our programs, to stop killing this important animal. And the flesh-eaters may wait a little until the cow dies. Then he gets the opportunity. Why there should be slaughterhouse maintained? As you are one of the leading citizens of Paris, we appeal to you to take up this consideration seriously. Why we should maintain slaughterhouse? If we want to eat the flesh, let us wait till the death. And there will be death. There is no doubt about it. So why they should maintain slaughterhouse? And this is most cruelty. A animal which is giving milk, so important foodstuff, and that is being killed, it does not suit any moral sense of any human being.
Srila Prabhupada (Room Conversation with Monsieur Mesman, Chief of Law House of Paris — June 11, 1974, Paris)

when the fossil fuels run out. A large family can meet all its requirement of energy and fertilizer from just two cows. Every home can be self-sufficient and grow energy in its own backyard.

Production techniques of various cow products should be made available on village level to make it a widespread cottage industry. Government can subsidize the machinery and investment just as it subsidizes slaughterhouses and beef production.

A nationwide awareness and consciousness has to be created. Citizens should vote for a political party which has cow protection in its agenda. All kingdoms in India set aside a portion of state outlay towards cow protection. Today's government is dedicating its resources for killing more and more cows.

Murder is one thing but a murder involving exceptional brutality or cruelty is a different thing altogether. For days and weeks on end, cows are piled on top of one another and shipped to far distant places. Most of them are injured and many die. Its long cruel road to the slaughterhouse. This is their final journey after a lifetime of service. This is the reward these innocent creatures receive after giving so much to the human race. These are the last frontiers of inhumanity. A public awareness has to be created against this barbarism and culprits should be brought to book. Cruel transport is illegal but the police is always hand in gloves with the butchers.

Cow is also a mobile temple. She is said to house the Supreme Lord and all the functional deities of material world. Cows and bulls are represented in all Hindu temples and home altars.

There is need for more seminars and workshops on the subject, both on local and international level.

If we examine the world history in last two thousand years, we find that all the revolutions were inspired by literature. There is need for more printed material on the subject to reach every home. Also there is need for more material for world wide web.

> *"Never doubt that a small group of thoughtful, committed people can change the world. Indeed, it is the only thing that ever has."*
> *- Margaret Head*

Things Can And Do Change With Efforts

A lot of things have been changed in this world with effort. There is no need to think that "nothing" can ever be done to stop the cruelty on cows and other animals.

Previously, there was no concern at all for animal testing on products, for example. The majority of people did not even know their products where being tested on animals.

Well, now they do. PETA called attention to it, and brought about enforced labeling on products that test on animals (among other things).

That's just a small example. Slavery used to exist in the world. Now, no one would even consider it. Something/someone changed it. It didn't just happen by itself. If enough people care and work together, anything can be changed.

It's like trying to turn the Titanic around, getting people to think of cow as friend, not food, but hopefully in the future it will be a thing of the past, like slavery and such.

THE AUTHOR

Dr. Sahadeva dasa (Sanjay Shah), is a monk in vaisnava tradition. Coming from a prominent family of Rajasthan, he graduated in commerce from St.Xaviers College, Kolkata and then went on to complete his CA (Chartered Accountancy) and ICWA (Cost and works Accountancy) with national ranks. Later he received his doctorate.
For close to last two decades, he is leading a monk's life and he has made serving God and humanity as his life's mission. His areas of work include research in Vedic and contemporary thought, Corporate and educational training, social work and counselling, travelling in India and aborad, writing books and of course, practicing spiritual life and spreading awareness about the same.
He is also an accomplished musician, composer, singer, instruments player and sound engineer. He has more than a dozen albums to his credit so far. His varied interests include alternative holistic living, vedic studies, social criticism, environment, linguistics, history, art & crafts, nature studies, web technologies etc.
His earlier books, Oil - A Global Crisis and Its Solutions (oilCrisisSolutions.com), End of Modern Civilization and Alternative future (WorldCrisisSolutions.com) have been acclaimed internationally. More information about his works is available on his portal DrDasa.com.

OTHER BOOKS BY THE AUTHOR

Oil - Final Countdown To A Global Crisis And Its Solutions

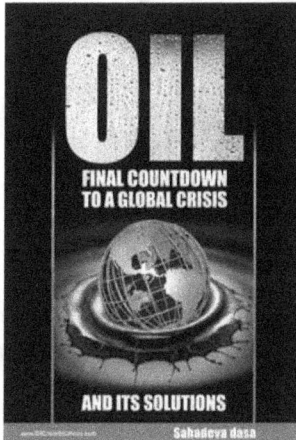

This book examines the lifeline of modern living - petroleum. In our veins today, what flows is petroleum. Every aspect of our life, from food to transport to housing, it is all petroleum based. Either it's petroleum or it's nothing. Our existence is draped in layers of petroleum. This book is a bible on the subject and covers every conceivable aspect of it, from its strategic importance to future prospects. Then the book goes on to delineate important strategic solutions to an unprecedented crisis that's coming our way. Pages-330   www.OilCrisisSolutions.com

ISBN 978-81-909760-0-8

End of Modern Civilization And Alternative Future

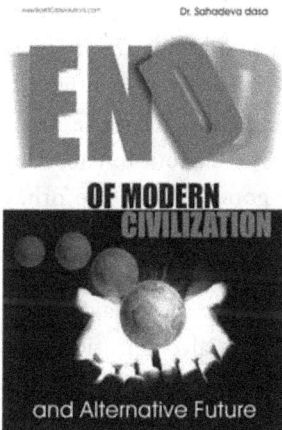

This book is an authoritative work in civilizational studies as it relates to our future. Dr. Dasa studied the human civilizations of last 5000 years and the reasons these civilizations collapsed. Each of them collapsed due to one or two factors like neglect of soil, moral degradation or leadership crisis but in our present day civilization, all these factors along with many more are operational. Then the book goes on to chalk out the alternative future for mankind. Pages-440   www.EndofCivilization.net

ISBN 978-81-909760-1-5

To Kill Cow Means To End Human Civilization

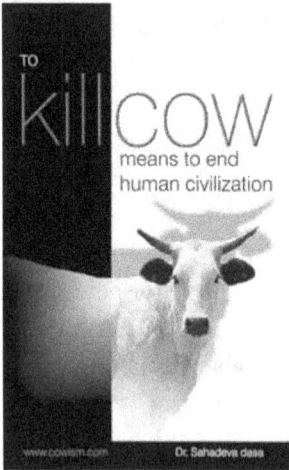

This landmark book on cow protection delineates various aspects of cow sciences as presented by the timeless voice of an old civilization. This book goes on to show that cow will be the making or breaking point for humanity. Science of cow protection needs to be researched further and more attention needs to be given in this area. Many of the challenges staring in the face of mankind can be traced to our neglect in this area.

Pages-136, www.cowism.com

ISBN 978-81-909760-2-2

Modern Foods - Stealing Years From Your Life

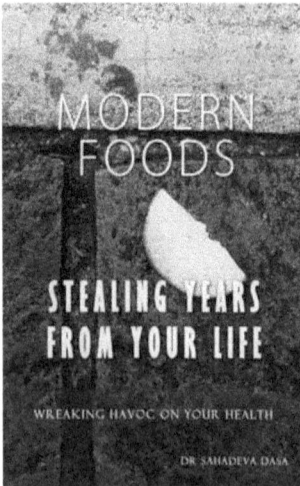

Food is our common ground, a universal experience. But there is trouble with our food. Traditional societies had good food but we just have good table manners. A disease tsunami is sweeping the world. Humanity is dying out. This is the result of our deep ignorance about our food. If you don't have good health, the other things like food, housing, transportation, education and recreation don't mean much. This books lists out major killer foods of our industrial civilization and how to escape them. It's a bible on the science of eating. Pages 330, www.farcefood.com, healthrealwealth.com

Cow Are Cool - Love 'Em

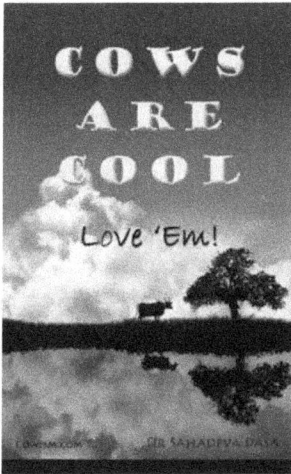

This book deals with the internal lives of the cows and contains true stories from around the world. Cow is a sober animal and does not wag its tail often as a dog. This does not mean dog is good and cow is food. All animals including the dog should be shown love and care. But cow especially has a serious significance for human existence in this world. Talk about cows' feelings is often brushed off as fluffy and sentimental but this book proves it otherwise.

Pages 136, www.cowism.com

ISBN 978-81-909760-4-6

Capitalism Communism & Cowism - A New Economics For The 21st Century

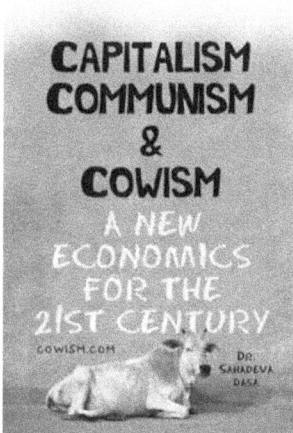

If humanity and the planet have to survive, we have to replace our present day economic model. It's a fossil fuel based, car-centred, energy inefficient model and promotes over exploitation of natural resources, encourages a throwaway society, creates social injustice and is not viable any longer.

This book presents an alternative economic system for the 21st Century. This economic works for the people and the planet.

Pages 172, www.cowism.com,
ISBN 978-81-909760-6-0

Noble Cow - Munching Grass, Looking Curious And Just Hanging Around

In Taiwan, a cow separated from owner, goes on hunger strike. In rural Cambodia, a motherless child finds mother in a cow as he suckles her. Down in Australia a flood heroine, after rescuing her owner, is leading a pampered existence. In Brazil's Pantanal swamps, a cow was seen wandering among the crocodiles while in India, the land of holy cows, a bull hero is booked out for two years. Up in Alps, the Swiss are combating stress by renting out the mountain cows while in Germany, the nation's focus has been on Yvonne, the runaway cow. There are numerous such stories here. Cows rule and cow rock! Pages 144, Cowism.com, ISBN 978-81-909760-8-4

Let's Be Friends - A Curious, Calm Cow

Normally we see cows as docile, dumb creatures, grazing nonchalantly in some far distance. But there is a whole lot more going on in their lives. Numerous stories from around the World are presented herein to substantiate this point.

Why do humans exploit and massacre each other so regularly? Why is our species so violence-prone? To answer these questions we would do well to think about our exploitation and slaughter of animals and its effect on human civilization.

Pages 136, Cowism.com,
ISBN 978-81-909760-9-1

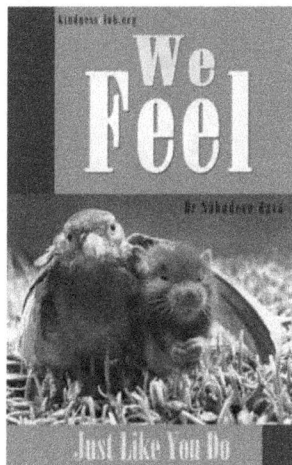

Its enormously puzzling that extreme suffering only gets widely questioned if it is the suffering of members of the human species. It is extraordinary how many people just accept the appalling treatment of such a vast number of animals.

Animals have souls and we have a duty to respect them! Anything less is to deny one's humanity and one's own soul!

Numerous stories outlined in this book prove this point, beyond the shadow of a doubt. Pages 144, KindnessClub.org ISBN 978-81-909760-7-7

www.ingramcontent.com/pod-product-compliance
Lightning Source LLC
Chambersburg PA
CBHW050349280326
41933CB00010BA/1388